THE

SOUTH ROAD

OTHER BOOKS BY ROBERT J. ADAMS

* * *

THE STUMP FARM

BEYOND THE STUMP FARM

HORSE COP

FISH COP

THE ELEPHANT'S TRUNK

SKUNKS AND HOUND DOGS

THE
SOUTH ROAD

To: Ruth:

Best wishes

[illegible] 2005

ROBERT J. ADAMS

MEGAMY

First published in 2001
2nd Printing 2002
Printed in Canada

THE PUBLISHER:
Megamy Publishing Ltd.
P. O. Box 3507
Spruce Grove, Alberta, Canada T7X 3A7
E-mail: megamy@compusmart.ab.ca

Canadian Cataloguing in Publication Data
Adams, Robert J., 1938–
The south road
ISBN 0-9681916-8-1

1. Adams, Robert J., 1938– —Anecdotes. 2. Farm life--Alberta–Anecdotes. 3. Canadian wit and humor(English) I. Title.

PS8551.D3224Z53 2001 C818'.5402 C2001-900386-2
PR9199.3.A29Z53 2001

Senior Editor: Kelly Hymanyk
Copy Editor: Natalie King
Design, layout, and production: Kelly Hymanyk
Cover: Rage Studios Inc.
Printing: Quality Color Press

DEDICATION

FOR MEGAN AND AMY
Thank you for providing Pa with the opportunity
to experience and relive the energy, exuberance,
and innocence of youth.

CONTENTS

DISCLAIMER

The stories you are about to read are all true. The men, women, and children you will read about are all people from my past. I have taken the liberty of changing the names of many of them to protect their identities. Although I view the past as being very humorous, they may not.

ACKNOWLEDGEMENTS

In the early 1940's when my parents, Bob and Florence Adams, bought a piece of land south of Edson, Alberta, no one ever dreamed it would be the setting for a book, let alone a series of books. I would like to thank my parents for providing our family with a good home, tons of love, and a lifestyle that built character and honesty.

Also, a big thanks to my siblings, Gwen, Larry, and Judy, for their childhood companionship and the fabulous memories that brought many of these stories to life—and for jogging my memory on many more.

I would especially like to thank my brother Larry for his friendship, his insight, and his unspoken loyalty.

I am grateful, as always, to my daughter Kelly for the countless hours she willingly gives, keeping me in check. Without her, this book would not have been written.

Thanks to Mar for her partnership in creating our own family stories. They may never find their way to print but I cherish them every bit as much.

INTRODUCTION

Robert Adams is a storyteller. He has the ability to tell his stories in a way that brings the past to life. His stories are charming and innocent. They are loved by Canadian readers, young and old, from all walks of life.

What makes Adams a favourite storyteller is that no matter what the age of the readers, his stories compel them to tell their own stories, to remember their own youthful experiences, and to share them with others. What greater gift can we give our children and our grandchildren than to share the past through our personal experiences.

His many readers thank him for sharing his stories and in turn, giving them the courage to tell their own. Future generations of Canadian readers will be grateful to him for recording our history in such a charming way.

MEGAMY PUBLISHING

THE

SOUTH ROAD

CABIN FEVER

Streaks. Long, shimmering, dancing streaks pierced the star-studded heavens. Like a paintbrush gone wild, the northern lights were dancing across the skies of western Alberta.

It was a bitterly cold night, following an equally bitterly cold day. It had snowed heavily for days before the skies cleared and the temperature plummeted. There was no sense looking at the thermometer to see how cold it was, because the little red line had crawled back into the bulb at the bottom.

A new, fresh, pure-white blanket of snow, almost a foot deep, lay on the top of previous snowfalls. It covered the trails. It covered all previous signs of life on the trails, on the walks, around the house, the well, and the outbuildings. Snow lay heavily on the branches of the spruce and the pine trees. Lower branches on the spruce trees were bent until they touched the ground; it was hard to tell where the branches ended and the ground began. To add to the misery of the snow and the cold, the north wind came a-calling. It was not a real howling wind, just a good stiff breeze, but it was unwelcome as it whispered and whistled through the trees. It swept through spruce and pines, lifting puffs of snow off the branches. The wind and the snow swirled into the clearing and around the log house. Snow filled in the walk, drifting high under the windows and around the door. The north wind drove the temperature ever lower.

A warm light glowed from a kerosene lantern hung in the middle of the kitchen. Its faint rays flickered through a frosty window into the cruel world outside. Inside, the Adams family, minus one, had just finished supper. It was a typical family scene in our house every evening all winter long. In the winter, Dad was away, working in the bush camps. His place sat empty until spring breakup, when he would return to the head of the table.

"Ah, yes," I crowed, as I patted my belly after a hearty meal. "As soon as you girls get the table cleaned off, I think I'll just work on the puzzle for awhile." Being the man of the house while Dad was away did have its advantages, I thought, as I leaned back on my chair and surveyed the kitchen.

The table, covered with an oilcloth, was strewn with dirty dishes. There was half a loaf of homemade bread, a butter dish with homemade butter in it, and an empty two-quart sealer that, prior to supper, had contained blueberries. On the back of the cookstove sat the teakettle, the coffee pot, and what was left of a huge pot of stew, all keeping warm. On the front of the stove, over the firebox, sat the dishpan full of hot water, just waiting for those dirty dishes. In the middle of the stove was the double boiler. It had been full of snow, but the snow was melting and was no longer visible.

"Before you get too comfortable, Bobby," Mom's voice jarred me back to reality, "you can get dressed and bring in another pail of water." Those words shattered my peaceful thoughts.

"What?" I snapped. "But . . . but I already brought in a pail of water."

"Well, we've used it all, and if you want breakfast in the morning I'll need more water."

"I don't want any breakfast in the morning," I mumbled.

"Well, I do," Mom said. "Now put your coat on and go fetch a pail of water before I get angry."

"But Mom, I . . . I already done my chores," I argued. "And it's really cold out there, too." How could I forget how cold it was—hadn't I walked home from school that day?

"You bundle up, boys, and you go straight home," the old janitor had said. He was warning every boy as we walked out of the boys' side of the red-brick schoolhouse. "It's a cold one out there, boys! She's a good 40 below if she's a degree. Don't you go wasting any time playing around, now, you hear?"

And it *was* cold. We really didn't need any warning not to dally. We walked away from the school, through town, along Highway 16, and down the South Road as fast as our little legs would carry us. As on every other day in mid-November, it was almost dark by the time we arrived home.

Larry and I had stayed in the house for only a few minutes, just long enough to start to feel the warmth from the cookstove and to drink in the smell of the stew, before we grudgingly turned and walked back into the cold. The path leading to the well and on to the barn was almost covered. Drifting snow, blown from the trees, had done its job. Only a faint shadow marked the way. We plowed forward, through the snow, down to the well. I found the axe leaning up against the fence and proceeded to chop ice out of the horse trough; then I hoisted up bucket after bucket of water and poured it into the trough.

Larry had gone on to the barn and brought the cows and the horse out. Steam poured off the backs of the animals as they stood in the cold to drink.

"Holy man, are these animals ever thirsty," I muttered to myself. "I bet I pulled twenty pails of water out of that well." After the animals were watered, we didn't have to coax them to return to the barn. They hustled back and moved right smart-like into their own stall. Each animal was given its share of hay and a helping of oats. Larry and I each grabbed a milk pail and a little stool, sat down under the business end of a cow, and began to milk.

Brrowrrrrpp came the sound of the first shot of milk to hit the bottom of the metal pail. Each time a hand squeezed and pulled a teat, a stream of milk shot down into the pail. Soon the *brrowrrrpp* was replaced by a rhythmic *swish-swish-swish,* the sound of a stream of warm milk cutting through the building head of foam before entering the milk at the bottom of the pail. We poured fresh, warm milk into the cat's dish. We mixed some milk into chopped feed for the old sow. We threw wheat to the chickens and gathered the eggs. Then Larry and I, carrying the milk and eggs, plowed our way through the snow back to the house.

But we were not yet finished. The old stoves, the cookstove and the airtight heater, both had to be fed, and on cold winter nights they ate a lot of wood. Larry and I plowed our way out to the woodshed. There, we took turns splitting dry spruce and pine and carrying it into the house. We filled the woodbox. We stacked firewood up against the wall. We piled firewood as high as we could reach, almost to the ceiling. We knew how hungry those stoves were, and we did not want to go out into the cold again on this night.

My last chore was a trip to the well, to fetch a pail of water. Larry took the double boiler outside and filled it with snow. He packed and heaped it up to a peak, well over the top of the rim. We hauled it in and hoisted it up onto the cookstove. Mom immediately grabbed the teakettle and poured the steaming contents into the double boiler.

"Why do you always do that?" I asked.

"If I don't add some water, I'll burn the bottom out of the tub," she replied. "And I can't afford to buy another one." Then she walked over to the water pail and with the dipper proceeded to fill the kettle again.

In the winter, snow was another source of water on

the Stump Farm. Mom preferred melted snow water for washing clothes—she said it was softer—and she always had a tub of snow melting on the stove. But now, after I had done all my chores, I was being asked to venture forth once more. It was unthinkable. Larry and I, we had done our chores.

"But Mom," I protested, "it's cold out there you know. And I . . . Larry and I, we already done our chores. Give somebody else a chance for some fresh air. Somebody else can get the water."

"It's not any warmer for anybody else," Mom replied. "Now, I'm not telling you again. Get on out there and fetch a pail of water. While you're outside, you might as well bring in some more snow to melt."

"Well, I suppose everyone else is just . . . just gonna sit around and do nothing while I hafta do all the work," I grumbled.

"There's lots of work for everybody," Mom said. "C'mon girls, get started on the dishes."

"I don't wanna do dishes," whined one of my sisters. "I did dishes last night and I'm not doing them again tonight."

"Well, I cooked last night, and I cooked tonight too, and you don't hear me complaining," Mom countered. "C'mon now, let's get our chores done, then we can all sit down for a few minutes. Larry, you can empty the slop pail."

The slop pail, a huge, five-gallon pail that sat on the floor by the cupboard, was the catch-all for everything that had to be thrown away. It was always dumped at the garbage pile out behind the outhouse. In the summertime, water was just tossed out the door, but in the wintertime, it went into the slop pail. During the winter, everything went into the slop pail and it became one sloppy, soupy, gooey mess.

"Why can't Rob dump the slop pail?" Larry asked. "He has to get dressed and go outside anyway."

"Don't argue with me. Empty the slop pail," Mom demanded.

Oh no, the Stump Farm was not a happy place. In every eye, tears were welling up, and they were not tears of joy. They were tears of misery as we all grudgingly prepared to tackle our next tasks.

"Now I got my socks wet," I grumbled as I picked up my boots and pulled them on. "I hope you're happy."

"If you got your socks wet, it's your own fault," Mom replied. "I told you to mop up around the door after you traipsed all that snow onto my floor."

"Moppin' the floor is girls' work," I yelled as I picked up the water pail and charged out, slamming the door behind me. I made several more trips outside, where I scooped up pail after pail of snow and hauled them in for Mom to dump into the double boiler.

Then, dragging the water bucket, again I plowed through the snow, heading for the well. I lifted the lid and grabbed the rope. I tied it onto the pail and dropped it down. Not even the stupid pail would co-operate on a night like this – it didn't fall right. It landed open side up and sat like a boat on the top of the water. I cursed loudly, for no one was around to hear me, as I hoisted the pail into the air and dropped it once again.

This time I gave the rope a flip and the top of the pail, the open part, hit the water first. As the water rushed in, the pail filled and sank. Then I hoisted it up and out of the well. I untied the rope and closed the lid.

There was no need to hurry, for I knew if I got back too soon, there would probably be another task waiting for me. For a moment, I enjoyed the peace and quiet. I stood by the well and stared at the house. The smoke from the roaring fire in the cookstove and the airtight heater billowed out of the chimney. The wind picked it up immediately and whipped it across the roof. Mixing with the blowing snow, it whisked over the eavestroughs. A mixture of smoke and snow twirled around the icicles adorning the entire length of the house, then plunged toward the ground, only to be swept up and swirled away. Away from the log house it blew, across the yard, zipping and darting among the trees; then it was gone, lost in the frozen night. The inside of the house did not know the harshness of the outside, for inside, Mom had kept it toasty warm.

I gazed up at the heavens, at the clear sky, the moon, the stars, the northern lights. I stood in awe of the northern lights, the changing hues of green, tinges of red, orange, yellow, and blue as they danced across the heavens. It was amazing that, amid all this snow and freezing cold, God had created so much beauty.

But I soon realized that standing there in the cold was worse than any chore. I suddenly felt a chill, clear to the bone. Forgetting the lights, I quickly picked up the bucket, lowered my head, and started forward. Once more, I cursed, for in the deep snow I had to lift the pail high, almost to my shoulders, so as not to spill the water. Now, with my head held high, standing up as tall as I could stretch, I slogged my way back to the house.

Inside our cozy little home, the mood had not changed. The dishes were gone from the table, but not all had been washed. They were stacked over on the cupboard top, by the kitchen window. The dishpan had been removed from the stove and was sitting beside the dishes. Steam billowed up from hot water, and the unhappy kitchen help were reluctantly, slowly, working on the pile.

I stomped the snow off my boots. I brushed the snow from the bottom of the bucket, then I hauled it over to the cupboard and plunked it down beside the dishpan.

"I'm not standing here and washing any more dishes. Robert's tracking snow and water all over the floor!" howled my sister. "Now my feet are wet, too."

"Bobby, get your boots off and mop up this floor," Mom scolded me. "Honestly, you'd think you were born in a barn. And you stay where you are until those dishes are finished," she said to a very unhappy Gwen.

"Moppin' the floor is girls' work," I mumbled. Then, I picked up the dipper and scooped a drink of the ice-cold water out of the water bucket. As I slurped down the water, I squinted through the heavily frosted pane. I looked towards the heavens for another glimpse of the northern lights.

"Man, is this window ever frosted!" I whistled as I moved my head around looking for a clear place on the glass. Jack Frost had made his appearance early this year. He had painted fancy designs on all the windows in the house. As usual, he started at the bottom of each windowpane, in the corners. He painted his flowery designs across the bottom and up the sides of the glass. In this freezing weather, the glass was almost covered. Yes, Jack Frost had done a number on our windows. In order to find a clear spot for a better look, I pushed in towards the centre of the window, into Gwen's space, and nudged her ever so slightly.

"What do you think you're doing?" she snarled at me.

"I thought I heard something outside," I whispered and pushed in a little more as I craned my neck for a glimpse of the northern lights.

"Not in this weather you didn't," she replied unhappily as she pushed back.

"I did too," I yelled back and pushed again. "I heard something out there."

"You're the only one that'd be dumb enough to go out on a night like this."

"That's enough, you two," Mom scolded. "Bobby, you get away from that window and you leave your sister alone. You know perfectly well there's nothing out there. I'm not telling you again to take your boots off and then mop up this floor."

"Moppin' is girls' work," I mumbled again. Then I shuffled back to the door and took my boots off.

"Bobby, mop the floor," Mom said angrily.

I ignored that order and deliberately plunked myself down in a chair and stared at her. To my surprise, the others stopped what they were doing and also sat down. That did it; Mom was beside herself. But before she could say another word, there was a noise outside our door.

BANG!

It sounded as though something, or someone, had just kicked the door. Then the doorknob rattled. I hadn't been serious when I said I heard something outside, but there definitely was something outside now. We all heard it and we all froze. We all stared at the door. No one moved. No one said a word. Boy, I'll tell you, I couldn't have said anything if I'd wanted to, for my heart had leapt right up into my throat. I was speechless. In fact, sitting in my chair, I was the closest one to the door, and I was scared stiff. I prayed that whatever was outside couldn't get inside.

The northern lights were still dancing across the heavens and the wind was whispering through the trees when the door suddenly flew open. Our hearts stood still. In a cloud of mist, the cold air and a dark figure burst into our home. I heard gasps from around the table before we all breathed a sigh of relief.

"I'll tell you, Girl, that's what I call a cold one!" Grandfather snorted as he turned and shut the door. He took off his hat and slapped his trouser legs, sending a shower of snow across the kitchen. Then he stamped his feet, and more snow—clumps of snow—skittered across the floor. Grandfather wasn't one to linger outside in the cold to rid his trousers and boots of snow. The amount of unwanted water on the floor was increasing rapidly.

"That's no weather to be out in. You know, Girl, it isn't fit for man nor beast out there," he said to Mom and laughed.

"Well, it's not fit for man nor beast in here, either," she replied. "Bobby, this is the last time I'm telling you—get the mop, and mop this floor."

"What's the trouble, Girl?" Grandfather asked.

"Cabin fever," Mom replied unhappily. "I think we've all come down with a good case of cabin fever."

"You know, Girl, that was hard work walkin' up here, plowin' through all that snow," he replied. Grandfather had a way of not hearing some things, and he ignored Mom's comment completely.

"You know, Boy, I'd say the snow is up to a well-digger's butt," he laughed. "And I'm about all tuckered out from plowing my way up here." Then he paused and looked at me sitting comfortably in my chair. "Here, Boy, give me your chair," he said. Man, I had to move fast, or I'm sure he would have sat on me. I jumped out of the way and was rewarded by sopping up more water with my socks.

"Will someone get the mop, and mop up that water before every sock in this house is wet?" Mom asked. But no one moved. They all looked at Grandfather, then at the wet floor, then at me.

"Don't look at me," I snorted.

"Bobby, you're up now, will you please get the mop?" Mom pleaded.

"Why do I have to do everything?" I grumbled. "That's girls' work. I'm the man of the house! Tell one of the girls do it."

"I'll girl's-work you, young man," Mom replied tersely. "Now you get the mop and do as you're told."

"Here, Boy," Grandfather said cheerily, almost like he was bestowing some great honour on me. "Just mop around my feet a little. I want to take my boots off, an' I don't want to get my feet wet."

Normally, I was happy to see Grandfather, but on this godforsaken night there were very few things that would have pleased me. Mopping up the snow and water around Grandfather's feet was not one of them. Grudgingly, I traipsed over to the corner of the room where the mop stood. I grabbed it and half-heartedly swished it through the snow and water around Grandfather's feet.

"I'm just about at my wits' end with these kids," Mom said to Grandfather as she poured him a cup of coffee.

For some reason, Grandfather was in a rather jovial mood for a man who had just plowed through snow up to a well-digger's butt for half a mile in 40-below weather. He didn't seem to notice as I mopped around his feet. Then he absent-mindedly lifted one big foot, with his boot still on, and stomped down, right on the mop.

"Well, you know, Girl," he said as if nothing had happened, although he was getting a big grin on his face, "it was such a dreary night, I sorta needed a little cheerin' up tonight, so I thought I'd just stop by to make sure you were all alive and well." Grandfather chuckled as he checked out the tears. "I thought maybe we could play a little cards or work on that puzzle."

I tugged at the mop handle, but Grandfather's boot held firm.

"I know a way you can cheer me up," Mom replied. "For starters, you can take these kids and give me some peace of mind."

"Your big foot's on the mop," I informed him and gave the handle another tug.

"Boy, have you finished that jigsaw puzzle yet?" Grandfather asked Larry. He ignored his boot and the mop.

Jigsaw puzzles occupied a fair amount of time during the long winter months. We all loved to work on jigsaw puzzles and would spend hours hunched over a puzzle on the table. There was always a partly-finished puzzle under the oilcloth. But tonight we hadn't been good and finished our chores, so there had been no puzzle. In fact, I think Mom was thinking more of bed than puzzles at that moment.

"No, we haven't," I snapped at him before Larry could answer. "And I haven't finished mopping either, because your big foot's on the mop." I tugged at the handle again.

"What do you say?" Grandfather chuckled. "Let's have a look at that puzzle and work on it for a while. Workin' on a puzzle is a good way to take your mind off your problems."

"I don't feel like workin' on no puzzle," I muttered. "Can you move your big foot? It's on the mop."

"Well, Girl, if we're not going to play cards or work on that puzzle," Grandfather said, shaking his head and looking genuinely disappointed, "I guess I'll be gettin' along." I figured Grandfather had been cheered up about as much as he could take for one day. He was getting out while the getting was good.

"Oh, by the way, Girl, have you seen anything or heard any strange noises?"

"Just these kids, why?" Mom sighed. Mom sure looked tired. "Just these kids."

"You know, Girl, I saw some strange-lookin' tracks in the snow," he said. "I thought they might be deer, but then it looked like there was a sleigh track too. You know, Girl, now that I think of it, it could be one of Santa's elves. The snow had drifted over the tracks and it was hard to tell, but you never know."

"Ha!" I laughed. "In this weather? I doubt it, Grandfather. Santa wouldn't send his elves out in this weather. They're used to working in a toy shop. They'd freeze to death."

"I don't know about that," he said shaking his head. "You be careful if you have to go outside tonight. You never know, Boy."

"Ha!" I snorted.

Then Grandfather stood up. He looked down at his boots and the mop.

"What the – " he exclaimed. "Did I have my foot on that mop? You should have said somethin', Boy. For goodness' sake, I'm sorry, Boy." He laughed. Then he stomped his feet again, sending more water onto the linoleum, before he opened the door and, singing to himself, disappeared in a cloud of mist.

He sees you when you're sleeping
He knows when you're awake
He knows if you've been bad or good
So be good for goodness' sake . . . .

We heard Grandfather singing until he slammed the door. And just like that, he was gone, into the freezing winter night. Not even Grandfather, who loved to kid around and joke, could bear another minute in our happy little home. Oh man, but we were a grumpy, miserable lot.

"Not much chance of him getting his socks wet," I grumbled. "He never even took his boots off." Then I took a last swipe at the floor. I dropped the mop and sat down. Who cared if my socks were wet?

Grandfather's short visit seemed to lift Mom's spirits a bit. She relented. The oilcloth came off the table, exposing an almost-completed jigsaw puzzle. The dishes sat unfinished. The floor was still wet. But we all turned our attention to the puzzle. We soon forgot about Grandfather and the miserable weather. The puzzle was almost finished and, as with every puzzle that was close to being finished, it became a terrible source of frustration. There were pieces missing.

"Someone's hiding pieces of the puzzle," said my sister Judy, and she cast me an accusing glare. "Robert, you always hide pieces of the puzzle. C'mon. Where are they?"

"Don't look at me," I grumbled back. "I was mopping the floor. Remember?"

"Well, someone's got them," she said.

It seemed that we could never complete a puzzle without a bit of confrontation, for someone always hid a piece or two. Sometimes even three. Everyone wanted to be the one to put the last piece in place. Personally, I always found it to be a source of great satisfaction to be the one to set the last piece in place and complete the puzzle. However, the puzzle at the end of that miserable day proved to be just one more thing to torment our touchy family. Voices rose. Accusations flew.

"That's it," Mom yelled. "I've had enough! Everyone's going to bed! Now!"

At that moment, outside the house, there was another noise. There was no banging or stomping of feet. It was a different sound, like something tiny on the side of the house or . . . or maybe even on the roof. Once again, the inside of the log house went deathly silent. We all held our breath and turned to stare out the frosted window.

Ping.

Like a bell, the sound rang through the night. It scared me so bad, I just about jumped right out of my skin. Was it a real bell or an icicle breaking away from the roof? We all held our breath and listened.

Ping . . . ping . . . ping . . .

I jumped again. It wasn't a bell—it was icicles, and they were breaking away from the roof.

"What's that?" someone asked.

"Shush," Mom whispered. She started to inch towards the window, but she stopped when the scratching sound started. Something was scratching on the logs right beside our window.

Then, through Jack Frost's painting, through his delicate designs, something moved. Whatever was outside scratching was now at our window. Suddenly Jack Frost's painting began to move and show some colour. The image took on all kinds of crazy shapes as it danced across Jack Frost's paintings. The image showed red and white, and it was not just outside the window, it was on the other side of the icicles. It was bobbing up and down, moving back and forth as if it was trying to see inside. We watched, silent, our mouths open, as it moved down, then came closer to the centre of the window. It was weird; I had never seen anything like it in my life.

"What is it, Mom?" I asked excitedly.

"I'm not sure," she replied.

Slowly, a pointed, red object took shape through the leafy designs. At the top was a white tassel. Suddenly, the object shot up to the small area not yet painted by Jack Frost. For a brief moment it stopped and peered through our window. A ruddy, whiskered face topped by a red cap and a white tassel appeared in our window, in the glow from the kerosene lantern. Just that quickly, it dropped out of sight and was gone.

Our mouths dropped and we all stared. Was it one of Santa's elves? Had an elf just looked through the window into the kitchen—at the table, the unfinished jigsaw puzzle, at the four squabbling, howling, fighting Adams kids?

"Was . . . was it one of Santa's elves?" I asked Mom. Everyone's eyes were on the window. All at once, I found my hand reaching into my trouser pocket and retrieving several pieces of the puzzle. I slipped them back on the table.

"I don't know," she replied.

"It was one of Santa's elves, wasn't it, Mom?" Larry asked.

"I don't know," Mom replied. "I've never had a good look at one of Santa's elves."

"It looked like an elf to me," I added quickly.

We all sat there, stunned by this strange turn of events. Suddenly, we came to our senses. We raced to the window for another glimpse of the elf. We were too late; there was no sign of Santa's elf. There was only the snow and the bitter cold. The elf was gone.

When I looked back at the puzzle, more of the missing pieces had mysteriously appeared on the kitchen table. We all wanted someone else to be the one to put the last piece in place, to take the glory for completing the puzzle.

But I had other things on my mind. I grabbed that mop and, girls' work or not, I mopped that floor. Like a wild man, I scrubbed and polished until there was not a flake of snow or a drop of water remaining anywhere.

"You sit down, Mom. I'll get you a cup of coffee," Larry warbled. He grabbed a cup and poured a coffee. Then he raced over to the stove and stoked the fire. He tossed another log into the airtight heater.

Gwen and Judy were over at the cupboard washing and drying the dishes.

"Let me help you, girls," I sang out. "I'll put the dishes in the cupboard for you."

In no time, the chores were done. Then we all sat down and finished the puzzle, and the oilcloth was returned to the table. No one had to be asked to do a chore. Eager hands tidied up the kitchen. Then a huge glass of milk and some cookies were placed at the centre of the table—just in case Santa's elf should return to the scene.

What a magical moment it was! Gone was the foul mood that had engulfed our cozy home. Suddenly, the Adams kids were the picture of goodness. If that was one of Santa's elves, he would know that there were only good little boys and girls in the Adams household. The elf was sure to send back a good report to Santa.

Outside, the northern lights shimmered and danced and streaked their way across the star-studded heavens.

"I sure wish Santa's elf would have been here before supper," Mom said. Then she smiled wearily as she tucked the four little angels into bed in their spotless, cozy cabin.

THE TOILET TYRANT

In the summer, the clay was either dried and baked to the consistency of the finest concrete, or it was wet, gooey, sticky, rubber-boot-eating gumbo. Depending on the weather, either definition could readily describe the yard surrounding the buildings on Grandfather's pig farm. To ensure safe passage from one building to the next, Grandfather had laid down a series of 2x10 and 2x12 pine planks. When it was wet, the wise kept their feet on the planks.

So it was that all planks led to and from the front door, the only door to the farmhouse. The main planks led along the front of the house, from the door to the well. Grandfather's well had a pump—there was no throwing a pail down his well when one had to fetch water. From here, more planks were used to reach other destinations. One string of planks led around to the back of the house to the outdoor toilet and continued along to the woodshed. Another string led to the cauldron where Grandfather boiled the pig feed.

On Grandfather's pig farm, scattered between the plank walkways, there were bones. Rib bones, ham bones, T-bones, leg bones, back bones, shoulder bones, blade bones—animal bones of all sizes and all shapes. There were bones in the pigpens, bones outside the pigpens, bones scattered around the cauldron, bones around the woodshed, bones around the toilet, and there were bones around the house. One could say there were bones everywhere. Yes, bones littered the clay around the farmyard.

Every day, Grandfather, sort of a recycler before his time, went to town to collect food for the pigs. He collected spoiled and damaged vegetables and fruit from the grocery stores; he collected meat, fat, trimmings, and bones from the meat markets; and he collected meal scraps from the restaurants. Collectively, these ingredients, along with a variety of grains, made up the brew he stewed in the cauldron. This boiled mash (slop, as we called it) was guaranteed to include bones. Bones that would be fed to the pigs. Bones that would be chewed, crunched, or broken, but rarely eaten. Many of those bones eventually found their way out onto the clay in Grandfather's yard.

During wet weather, one never seemed to notice the bones. I know I didn't. I was always too busy concentrating on keeping my feet on the planks. Those old bones just settled into the clay, the top sides getting washed clean in the rain. When the sun shone and baked the clay, it also baked and bleached the bones. A farmyard full of sun-baked, bleached bones was an excellent place for a curious young boy. Especially a curious young boy with a good right arm.

It was on one nice, sunny summer afternoon that my brother Larry and I walked with Mom from the Stump Farm down to Grandfather's pig farm. There, Larry and I were treated to a healthy helping of Ma's oatmeal-and-date cookies. Each of those cookies was about the size of a wagon wheel. It took two glasses of lemonade to wash just one of them down.

"You boys go on outside and play," Mom said. "I want to talk to Ma for a minute."

"What are we gonna do?" I asked. "There's nothing to do outside." Actually, there was always lots to do, but it was a real hot day, and we knew Mom was itching to talk to Ma. It was a secret, and we were curious. We figured it would be better to stay inside, with our ears open and our mouths full. Where better to spend a hot summer day than close to Ma's cookie jar?

"Outside," Mom replied. "And don't go too far. We'll be going home shortly."

Reluctantly, Larry and I left Mom and Ma at the kitchen table. We dragged our feet out into the yard. The clay was baked. It was as hard as concrete. We kicked a few bones that were lying around the front of the house. Then we ambled over to an old swing that Grandfather had built. It was there that Mother Nature called. I made a beeline for the toilet. To my surprise and dismay, I discovered that the door was locked, from the inside. Up to that point, I had thought that Larry and I were the only two people about, except for

Ma and Mom back in the kitchen. That was obviously not the case.

"Hurry up in there!" I yelled. "I gotta go, real bad."

Out in front of the toilet, on the hard-baked clay, I waited. I crossed my legs and waited. I did a little nervous dance and waited. I kicked a few bones and waited. I picked up a few bones and tossed them at the woodshed and waited. Nothing was working—whoever or whatever was in that toilet was not getting out.

"Yo, you there in the toilet. Hurry up in there," I called out again. "Other people have to use the toilet too, you know."

"It doesn't look like there's anybody in there, Rob," Larry said. "Maybe the door's just stuck. Are you sure you checked it good?"

"I thought I did," I moaned. I had to go pretty bad, so I hotfooted it over to the biffy one more time. I grabbed the doorknob and yanked on it, but the door held fast and remained shut. I cocked my head to one side and listened carefully, but I heard not a sound. I could not detect any movement.

"Who's in there?" I called out and listened again. "Whoever you are, please hurry! Hurry, or I'm comin' in. I'll sit on your lap and do number two." But my plea and threat went unheeded. There was still no reply and no sound. Larry and I stood back and eyed the old toilet.

It was spooky. Normally, a person did not dally in an outdoor biffy. Especially a person in his right mind, on a hot, sunny afternoon. But someone or something was in there. Whoever or whatever it was, it was not moving. Meanwhile, I was in agony.

"What do you think?" I asked Larry.

"Beats me," he replied. "I'd say it's probably asleep—or dead."

"I think I'll see if I can wake him up," I said. I picked up a nice rib bone from the baked clay. I measured the distance to the biffy and decided that I should back up a bit, because even in my condition, with my legs almost crossed, I could throw a long way. I had a pretty good arm. I kept my eyes on the toilet door and backed away. Larry followed. When I reached what I guessed was the right distance, I reared back and tossed the rib bone.

Now, throwing a rib bone isn't like throwing a rock. That stupid bone flew through the air end over end, then did a little dipsy-doodling, before fluttering to the ground well short of the biffy.

"Rib bones don't throw too good," I mentioned to Larry.

Larry selected a very fine-looking rib bone, then he measured the distance very carefully and took aim. With all his might, he flung that bone towards the biffy and watched in awe as it, too, flipped and dipped before dropping to the clay short of its target.

Obviously, rib bones were meant to be thrown shorter distances. We moved closer and threw more rib bones. The odd rib bone found its mark and clunked off the wooden toilet door before plopping to the ground. In our attempts to dislodge the biffy incumbent, the baked clay within throwing distance of the toilet had been picked clean of rib bones. There was not a rib bone to be had. The baked clay and the planks right out in front of the toilet door, however, were now littered with sun-bleached rib bones.

I had to get access to that toilet. I picked my way through the rib bones, tiptoed up to the door, and grabbed the door handle. Hoping against hope that it would open, I gave it a quick yank. It wasn't about to move.

This wasn't funny. This was war.

I backed away and grabbed the first bone I laid my hands on. Suddenly, bones of all descriptions were flying. There were T-bones, round bones, ham bones, and leg bones. Some flew much better and straighter than others. There was a steady clattering of bones on wood and bones on sun-baked clay. Bones rained off the old toilet. Bones covered the baked clay and hid the planks around the front of the toilet.

But still we had not succeeded in unseating the biffy-squatter. The toilet door remained closed and locked—from the inside.

"Whoever's inside has to be dead," I finally said to Larry. "Nobody could sleep through all the bone-banging racket."

That nothing came out of the toilet did not dissuade us from throwing bones. The bones were getting bigger all the time. Now, I can tell you, it's not an easy thing to throw big bones, and it's even more difficult if you're trying to keep your legs crossed at the same time. But nothing will stop a man on a mission, and I was on a mission. I had to get into that toilet.

We ranged farther away to collect bones and then carried them closer to the target. We were down to tossing the big, burly ends of the leg bones. Each time a big bone banged off the door of the toilet, the whole biffy would rattle.

"There can't be anybody in there," Larry observed, after numerous bones had rattled the building. "There's got to be something wrong with the door."

"I checked it," I replied. "It's locked from the inside."

"Well, I think you're right—if anybody's in there, he's gotta be dead," he said. "Either that or his smeller don't work. The stink in there would knock a skunk off a gut pile." Then he reared back and lofted another big bone at the door.

"Hey, lookit this one," I called out. I had found a particularly large bone over by the woodshed. "This thing looks like a boomerang. I betcha if I miss the toilet, this old bone will come right back to me."

"Naw, it's too big and flat," he replied.

"Yeah, you're right," I muttered. "Anyway, it's probably too heavy to fly too far."

"Boy, I'll bet if that bone hits the toilet roof, it'll probably cave in. I'll bet everything in there will fall right through the toilet hole, Rob. Whoever's in there is going to get a big surprise when he finds himself in the hole!" Larry laughed. Then we both laughed.

It was a heavy old bone, and I took a few more steps closer to the toilet. I didn't want to miss the target with that prize. I reared back and, with all my might, I fired a two-hander high into the air. The big, flat bone sailed skyward. I was aiming for the roof. I watched as it rose upward, up above the roof, towards the sky. It made a beautiful arc and began its descent.

"Ah, darn," I muttered. "It's gonna fall short." I watched as the big bone plunged downward, short of the roof.

At that very instant, there was a squeak. Larry and I both stopped dead. We looked at the toilet. At the door. At the rusty hinges. My jaw dropped. The door to the toilet opened, a teensy-weensy bit. Had all the bones finally jarred the door open? Then I really got a surprise. Out of the door popped a head. It was about waist-high and it wasn't a dead head. It was a head with a smile on it, a big old silly smile. Two laughing, mocking eyes were looking right at me, enjoying my obvious discomfort. But those eyes should not have been looking at me. They should have been looking up. Up where that big, heavy, flat shoulder-blade bone was rapidly plunging earthward.

Now, Larry and I had heard the various sounds of bones—small bones, big bones, flat bones, round bones, and rib bones—rattling off dry, cured, stinky toilet-house wood. And we had heard the sounds of those bones bouncing off hard, sun-baked clay. We had heard the sound of those bones falling on planks. Why, we had even heard the sound of sun-bleached bones hitting sun-bleached bones. But we had not heard the sound of a huge, heavy, sun-dried shoulder-blade bone hitting a real live, hair-covered head bone. And I can tell you, there is no sound quite like it.

THUNK!

"Ooh man, that's gotta hurt," I moaned. I scrinched my eyes, pursed my lips, and gritted my teeth. The sound of the flat shoulder-blade bone meeting the round head bone was not as loud as the other sounds, but oh my goodness, it was sickening. The sound seemed to explode in my ears.

The big flat bone bounced off the head bone with the smiling face, it clunked off the dried wood of the toilet door, then it rattled onto the pile of bones covering the baked clay. It sounded like someone shaking dice before it found its resting place.

Quicker than it had popped out, the head disappeared. It just seemed to sort of drop and fall back into the toilet. The toilet door hung open for a second. Once more the hinges squeaked, and the toilet door lazily swung shut. Larry and I just stood and stared at the toilet. It was eerily quiet. It was like a morgue.

"Holy cow! Did you see that?" I asked Larry when I was finally able to speak.

"Yeah," Larry replied. His eyes were wide open and glued to the spot where the head had disappeared behind the closed door.

"Man, if he wasn't dead before, I'll bet he's dead now. Do you think I killed him?" I asked. But before Larry could reply, I had my answer.

Suddenly the toilet door exploded, flung open so fast that the old, rusty hinges never had a chance to squeak. The door swung wildly. It slammed against the side of the wall, pulling squeaking, squawking, protesting, rusty screws from old, dried wood. The bottom screws could not take the jolt. The hinges squawked one last time, and rusty old screws and splinters of wood scattered onto the pile of bones. The top screws held, and one corner of the toilet door sagged, then it too plunged onto the pile of bones.

Finally, the inside of the toilet was revealed. Standing in the doorway, holding one hand on the exact place where the flat shoulder blade had bounced off his noodle, was the toilet tyrant. A nincompoop who thought it was funny to monopolize the toilet while I waited in agony. He hesitated, as his eyes focused. Then he fixed mean, angry eyes, eyes filled with fire and hatred, on me.

"I'm gonna tear you apart, limb from limb!" roared the tyrant. He burst from the toilet like a raging bull. His first step was right into the pile of sun-bleached bones. His eyes showed shock and surprise as his foot floundered. Bones rattled and scattered in every direction. Down he went in a heap.

I didn't think it would be wise to wait around for him to congratulate me on my good arm and even better aim. And I certainly wasn't going to offer to help him up. My head told me that if I valued my life, I had better get my feet moving—and fast. I knew where safety lay, and it was not in front of the toilet. Mother Nature's call wasn't nearly as urgent as it had been—it was going to have to wait. I would just keep my legs crossed while I visited with Mom and Ma in the kitchen.

"Run for your life!" I yelled at Larry when I saw the tyrant scramble to his feet.

The last thing I saw as I turned and bolted for Ma's

front door was the toilet tyrant catching his foot on a plank. He hung suspended in the air, his arms suddenly flailing wildly, then once more he crashed into his bonedom. Amid the clattering of his subjects, I heard an angry curse. It didn't take a brain surgeon to tell me that I was a dead man if he ever got his hands on me. The next rib bones to be thrown at the toilet could be mine.

I put my head down, and as fast as my little legs could move, I ran past Grandfather's pump. I grabbed the pump handle to help me change directions and I aimed for the front door. Through the front door I raced. I zipped around Ma's chair and scooted in behind Mom.

"Outside," Mom said and pointed to the door. "I told you to wait outside while I'm talking to Ma."

"Save me, Mom!" I yelled, all out of breath. "You gotta save me!"

"Save you from what?" Mom asked.

"From . . . from the toilet tyrant, Mom! And . . . and the bones!" I panted. "There's bones out there, an' they're fallin' from the sky!".

BARNYARD COURT

"I'm telling you, Boy, I'm gonna git to the bottom of this," I heard Grandfather tell Dad one evening. "Everybody's comin', everybody. First we're gonna talk turkey, and then Ma's gonna cook us up a chicken supper." I had just come in from doing chores and had missed most of the conversation, but I didn't miss the important part.

"Hot dog!" I exclaimed. "We're gonna go to Ma's for a chicken supper." Grandfather stopped talking and they both looked at me. "My chores are done! I'm ready! What are we waiting for? Let's go!"

"Hold your horses, Boy," Grandfather replied.

"You mean we're not going to your place and there's not going to be a chicken supper and . . . and we're not gonna talk turkey either?" I mumbled. What had started out to be quite an exciting prospect had suddenly taken a disappointing turn.

"Sunday, Boy. On Sunday we're gonna talk turkey and then we'll eat chicken," Grandfather replied seriously.

"Whoopee!" I yelled, for all was not lost.

"Okay, we'll be there," Dad chuckled. Dad didn't seem to be nearly as excited as I was, but then Dad never seemed to get too excited about most things. He was level-headed and as solid as a rock.

Finally, Sunday arrived.

"Awright!" I whooped. Then I raced ahead, leading the way down the driveway. Mom, Dad, Larry, Gwen, Judy, and I—the entire family—were headed for Grandfather's place, and I was sure excited.

"C'mon, you slowpokes. What are you waiting for? C'mon!" I hollered again. "We don't want to miss out on the turkey and the chicken."

Man, I'll bet I ran every step, all the way from the Stump Farm to Grandfather's pig farm. I guess it would be fair to say that I was a keener. But then, I also knew that Ma was cooking, and I figured that she was about the best cook in the whole world. Nobody in his right mind would ever be late or miss a meal that Ma cooked. I certainly didn't want to miss out, and I raced ahead of the rest of my family. They had only walked about halfway when I, huffing and puffing, turned in at Grandfather's place.

"C'mere, Boy," Grandfather called to me. "You can give me a hand."

"You bet, Grandfather," I panted happily.

My lungs were burning like crazy and I would just as soon have rested, but not now. Not when I had a chance to work with Grandfather. Oh yes, it was always a proud moment in my life whenever I could help Grandfather. He was always the centre of attention, and whoever helped him usually got just as much attention as Grandfather commanded. Now, here I was, hardly in the yard and already I had been summoned. Yeah, I chuckled to myself, I'll probably be his right-hand man when he starts talking turkey.

Grandfather was busy down by the chicken coop. He had made a makeshift table using a couple of sawhorses with an old graindoor laid across the top of them.

"Well, come on, Boy," he called impatiently.

"I'm here, Grandfather," I panted. "I ran all the way from our house." I leaned over and put my hands on my knees to catch my breath.

"Well then, don't just stand there, Boy," Grandfather said seriously. "You just git back on your horses, and run over to the shed and get me a hammer and a piece of chain."

I searched through so much junk in that shed. There were scraps of metal, pieces of old harness, hunks of leather, lengths of belting, tires, and parts for cars all scattered around on the floor, hanging on the walls, and stacked on the workbench. There was everything imaginable in that shed. Everything but a length of chain and a hammer. I came out of the shed about the same time as the rest of my family walked into the yard.

"There's . . . there's no hammer or chain in the shed," I reluctantly informed Grandfather. He had just finished setting up a row of hay bales between the makeshift table and the chicken coop.

"You sit there an' hold those bales down, an' don't you move 'til I git back. There's been enough stuff movin' around here lately," Grandfather snorted, pointing at the row of bales. Then he stomped off towards the shed. He wasn't in there very long before he emerged carrying a huge ball-peen hammer and dragging about thirty feet of logging chain. He laid the hammer on the table, right in the middle, and then proceeded to coil the chain on one end.

"Are we gonna talk turkey now, Grandfather?" I asked.

"We are, Boy. Just as soon as everyone gets here," he replied. Grandfather was not in his usual jovial mood. He didn't seem to be unhappy, but he was all business as he prepared for the turkey talk.

"And then are we gonna have chicken for dinner?"

"That's right, Boy, then we'll have that chicken dinner Ma's cookin' up."

It wasn't long before Grandfather's yard was full of people. It seemed to me that he had invited everybody over to his place to talk turkey and eat chicken. Grandfather loved a crowd. He was always at his best when there were a lot of people around. I was just as excited as all get-out as I impatiently waited for the turkey-talking to begin. This was going to be a day to remember.

"C'mon, I want everyone down by the chicken coop," Grandfather called. I think every kid there was as anxious as I to talk turkey with Grandfather. We all raced for the chicken coop. I already had a good seat, right in the middle of the row. Right where Grandfather had told me to sit. Soon, there were kids sitting on the bales, standing on the bales. Some were standing on the ground, some had even gone into the chicken coop. Larry was sitting on a bale right beside me.

"C'mon now. I want all the kids sitting on the bales," Grandfather yelled out. He had a devilish smile on his face. As quick as a wink, it seemed every little butt in the farmyard was planted on a bale. And every little mouth was jabbering excitedly.

"Let's hurry up and talk turkey so we can git to that chicken!" I hollered above the chatter of little voices.

Grandfather, in full control now, stood behind the makeshift table. He was warming to the situation at hand. The rest of the adults stood around behind him. They were all bit players, even Ma, who had spent most of the day cooking the chicken supper. Then, without any warning, Grandfather picked up that big ball-peen hammer and slammed it down on the tabletop.

BAM. BAM. BAM. BAM.

Grandfather hit the top of that table hard and fast. Four blows of the hammer in rapid succession. Chunks of dried mud and dirt exploded from the old graindoor. With each blow of the hammer, clouds of dust billowed up. From little cracks in the boards, grains of wheat suddenly appeared and danced across the tabletop.

"Whew!" Grandfather coughed and flapped his free hand wildly, trying to wave the dust away. Through the dust I could see the hammer in his hand, waving about over his head. His grin had got more sinister-looking. I wasn't sure whether this was the way you talked turkey or not, but it had certainly got my attention, and everyone else's. In fact, he about scared the wits right out of all of us.

"Now, I want you kids to listen closely to what I have to say!" Grandfather roared. Then the hammer dropped again.

BAM. BAM. BAM.

The old ball-peen hammer pounded on the graindoor. More chunks of dirt, clouds of dust, and grains of wheat erupted from the tabletop.

"Now, you kids, you listen up!" he roared and flapped his free hand. "We're gonna talk some turkey here today. This is a court we're holdin'. An' I'm the judge!" Grandfather grinned and deliberately took the time to look at every kid sitting on a bale. "Now, do you all know what a court is?"

No one said a word. We all sat motionless, as if our butts had been glued to the hay bales. Our jaws had dropped, our mouths hanging open as if we were trying to catch flies. Every eye was wide open, and every eye was on Grandfather, his smile, and that big ball-peen hammer.

"I think it's more like a barnyard court," I heard one of the adults snicker.

"There'll be no talkin' in my court unless I say so!" Grandfather roared so that half the country could hear him. Then he continued.

"Now, this is a court. A court of law," he said slowly, looking from face to face. "Courts are set up to find out things. That's what we're gonna do here today. We're gonna find out what's been happinin' here—right here in my farmyard. There's been some funny things goin' on around here lately, and I want to hear all about it. Remember, this is a court," Grandfather repeated, "and I'm the judge. Now, I know that nobody here would lie, not to me. Not to the judge. I know that you're all honest. And in this court, this is the time for honesty, a time for everyone to speak the truth. Now, who wants to be first? Which one of you kids is gonna tell me what's bin goin' on around here when I'm not home?"

No one wanted to talk. Not a word was spoken. All eyes were on Grandfather and that big old ball-peen hammer that was sailing around his head. Suddenly, the hammer smashed to the table again.

BAM.

"What about you, Boy?" Grandfather said, pointing that hammer right at me. "I'll just bet that you got somethin' you want to tell me? Don't you, Boy?"

Man, my heart jumped into my throat. I had to swallow real hard to keep it from jumping right out of my mouth. Immediately, my thoughts raced back to the previous weekend . . . .

It wasn't just me, it was Larry and me. It all began very innocently, when we had gone down to Grandfather's place for a little visit and some of Ma's great oatmeal-and-date cookies. There was nobody at the house, though, so we moseyed on down to the barn and the pigpens. There was nobody at the pigpens either.

"Hey, Rob," Larry asked as we stood in front of the

pigpens, "whaddaya say we have some fun with the pigs?"

"Fun! With a bunch of stupid pigs?" I asked. "Are you daft or something?"

"Sure, I'm daft. C'mon," he urged. "Pigs can be a lot of fun. I'll show you."

"Oh sure," I scoffed. "Let's roll around in the mud with a bunch of dumb pigs. That really sounds like a lot of fun to me."

"C'mon, first we hafta get a couple of pails and pretend we're gonna feed the pigs," Larry said.

"Whoop-de-doo," I said. "Let's have a ball. Let's get some pails and feed the pigs. That oughta be a hoot."

"No, we're just gonna pretend," he explained. "Then, when they come up to the trough, we can ride them."

"You can't ride a pig," I laughed. "Who ever heard of riding a pig, anyway? That's dumb."

"Sure you can ride a pig," he replied. "I ride them all the time when Grandfather's not home. C'mon, you follow me an' I'll show you how it's done."

"Yeah, sure you will," I mumbled. I have to admit, I was pretty skeptical, but I followed along. We each got one of the pails that Grandfather used to feed the hogs, then we raced over to the troughs.

"Sow-pig, sow-pig," Larry called. I watched as he rattled his pail on the wire. I thought I saw him flinch, but he kept right on rattling and calling.

"Sow-pig, sow-pig, sow-pig," I called. Then I, too, laid my pail on the wire and rattled it.

"Yeow!" I screamed, and my pail flew from my

hands. That's when I found out Grandfather's electric fencer was turned on. As soon as the pail touched the wire, I got a jolt that sent tingles all the way up my arm. It was not the first time I had felt the shock of the electric fencer. I was used to it. Sometimes, I would even hold onto the wire to trick someone into thinking that it was turned off. But this time, I was caught off guard and got a good surprise. Larry, the little bugger, had got me good.

"Oh yeah, Rob," he chuckled, "I forgot to tell ya—ya gotta watch out for the electric shock."

"Thanks for nothin'," I muttered, and picked up my pail.

Well, those big fat old sows never fell for the empty-pail trick—they must have known that it was not feeding time. But the young pigs, about half-grown, were only about half-smart. Any pail-rattling around the fence at any time was feeding time to them. Before my pail even hit the ground, there were little pigs running from every direction. They charged through the trees, were squealing as if they had been stuck with a knife. They stuck their noses into the trough. They grunted and they squealed, they pushed and they fought, each one thinking that the others were getting all the food.

While the pigs were all busy trying to find out which one was hogging the food, Larry dropped his pail like a shot, and climbed over the fence. He never even broke stride as he hopped on the back of a pig.

Larry's pig was squealing like crazy as it raced, with Larry on its back, away from the troughs. I had never paid attention to the row of stumps, about eighteen inches high, that were between the troughs and the trees. But Larry knew they were there. He lifted his legs as his pig charged forward, zipping and zagging through the stumps heading for the trees.

"Yahoo, ride 'em pigboy!" I yelled. Larry was right, riding pigs did look like fun. And it looked easy too.

As fast as I could, I followed Larry over the fence. I selected the next pig and hopped aboard. I quickly found out that I didn't know nearly as much about pig-riding as Larry did. I should have asked what I was supposed to hang onto, because I quickly realized that my pig had no handles. My pig was moving, fast, and there was nothing to grab hold of.

"Reach around and grab his neck," a voice seemed to yell in my ear, but I was too late. That stupid pig spun. He went around so fast, he fired me off his back like an arrow. Straight into the ground. I landed face-first in the mud and pig poop.

"Ain't this fun, Rob?" I heard Larry laugh. Then I heard the pail-rattling back at the fence again. I looked up. Larry was back at the fence, and there were pigs at the trough. Those dumb pigs were still grunting and squealing. Still pushing and shoving. Still looking for the food they'd never find.

"Oh yeah," I muttered, covered in mud and pig poop. "This is real fun."

By the time I scrambled to my feet, Larry was heading through the trees on another squealing pig. There were pigs all around me and, without even thinking, I jumped the closest pig. This time, I found the handles. I grabbed and got a good hold on its ears. For a second, my pig just stood there and squealed — then it turned and took off, following Larry and his pig. Squealing bloody murder, it charged through stumps that were, I painfully learned, just about up to my knees. I think a knee bounced off every stump before that stupid pig darted into a clump of spruce trees. Twisting and turning, it ducked and dodged between branches and tree trunks. My pig raced out of the trees. I, on the other hand, lay flat on my back, my body twisted like a pretzel, half wrapped around a spruce tree.

"Isn't that fun?" Larry laughed. "C'mon, Rob, let's go get another one."

"Let's not, and say we did," I moaned. "I think I've had enough pig-ridin' for one . . . ."

BAM. BAM. BAM.

The old ball-peen hammer pounded again and jarred me back to talkin' turkey with Grandfather. I was scared spitless. My mouth was about as dry as a popcorn fart, and I had just about mustered up enough courage to speak. It was me, Larry and me — we were the ones Grandfather was looking for. We were the ones causing Grandfather all his grief. But I was the oldest. I would confess to my sins. I'd take the blame. I opened my mouth and tried to form the words.

"Now, I've told you kids, this is a court, and I'm gonna git to the bottom of what's goin' on around here. Okay now, I want to know which one of you has been stealing from me?" Grandfather's voice roared again, stopping me before I could speak out. His smile was almost gone now—almost but not quite. It was sort of a half-smiling, half-serious look he was wearing. Grandfather was really enjoying himself.

"Stealing," I said, but no words came out. "Stealing?" That was a word that surprised me. Riding the pigs wasn't stealing. Then it hit me, he doesn't know about the pigs. But how did he find out about the chicken? Once more, sitting on that hay bale in the barnyard courtroom, my mind wandered . . . .

"What're we gonna do now, Rob?" Larry asked, after I had dragged my aching, bruised body away from the spruce trees and out of the pigpen.

"I don't know," I mumbled. "But I don't think I can take another beating like that. I think we should try to find something a little more our size."

About that time, a chicken squawked over at Grandfather's chicken coop. Well, we didn't need anybody to tell us that a chicken was more our size—and besides, riding those pigs had been hard work. Larry and I had worked up quite an appetite.

"What do you say to a nice feed of fresh chicken, roasted over an open fire?" I asked.

"Yeah! That sounds good to me," Larry chuckled, excited at the thought. "You know, Rob, I don't think that dumb chicken is gonna see nightfall."

The chicken was harder to catch than the pigs. We chased that squawking, flapping bird all around the barnyard before we finally caught it. Once we got our hands on it, though, it was a whole lot easier to hold onto than the pig.

"You hang onto the chicken, and I'll get some matches," I said. I raced into the house and found a big box of wooden matches. Sometimes, fires can be hard to start in the muskeg, so I took a handful. Larry gave me quite a start when he showed up at the door with the squawking, gawking chicken in his hands.

"Bring some paper too, Rob," he said. "We'll need it to start the fire."

"How about this?" I asked, holding up a shopping bag.

"That'll do," he replied. Then we raced out of the house with all the fixin's we needed for roasting our chicken—a match, a paper bag, and one chicken.

We stopped at the woodshed, and on the chopping block the chicken lost its head. I picked it up, and when we raced past the pigpen, I tossed it in. No sense letting a good chicken head go to waste, I thought, as one of the stupid pigs finally found something to eat. He chomped it down. We ran past Grandfather's barn and out into the muskeg. We left a trail of chicken feathers from the barn out to where we picked a spot to light a fire. Larry gathered some old man's beard, tree moss, and a bunch of dead spruce branches. Then, with the help of a good portion of the shopping bag, he soon had a rip-roaring fire going.

I used my jackknife, my squirrel-skinning knife, to cut the legs and the breast meat off the bird. Then we cut some willow shafts and sharpened them at both ends. On one end of each shaft, we skewered a piece of chicken. Then we jammed the other end into the muskeg, leaving the chicken dangling in the flames. There was nothing to do now but sit back and wait for our feast.

It didn't take but a few seconds for us to realize that we should have skinned those pieces of chicken. At least, we should have done a better job of plucking them. As soon as the flames hit the feathers we had missed, they started to burn. Instantly, the air was filled with a smell that was worse than pig poop. We beat a hasty retreat through the muskeg, quickly moving upwind, back into the trees, giving our roasting chicken a wide berth.

"Phew," I coughed and gagged. "Does that ever stink! I'm glad chicken doesn't stink like that when Mom cooks it."

"Let's make us a smoke, Rob," Larry said. "That'll take our mind off the smell."

"A smoke!" I replied. "How we gonna do that? We got no tobacco and we got no papers."

"I'll show you, Rob. Old man's beard and brown paper," he laughed. "We can smoke old man's beard."

Larry plucked some of the moss from the tree. Then he tore two chunks of the brown paper from the remains of the shopping bag. Like an expert, he rolled some of the moss into one of the pieces of paper and handed it to me. Then he rolled one for himself. He didn't even use a match to light his. He walked back through the stink and, like an old pro, he pulled a burning twig out of the fire.

"Here ya go, Rob," he warbled as he held the twig up for me. I followed him to the fire. The feathers were just about all gone, burning off the pieces of chicken, and the stink was definitely fading. I lifted my homemade roll-yer-own to my lips and he touched it with the flame. The old man's beard flared up and the brown paper bag started to burn. I quickly sucked in a big breath. Instantly, the old man's beard inside the brown paper was fire from one end to the other. My mouth was full of smoke and flame and the most incredibly horrible taste. I gagged, then I coughed and spit. I threw the whole works into the fire.

"They're a little strong, aren't they, Rob?" Larry wheezed. "I don't think you're supposed to try to smoke them all at once." Tears filled his eyes and streamed down his cheeks. But Larry is a tough one. I couldn't believe my eyes when once more he lifted his roll-yer-own to his lips. He took a very small drag and another flood of tears filled his eyes.

"They're too strong for me," I croaked. "I think I'll just wait for the stinkin' chicken."

"Hey, Rob, where'd the chicken go? What happened to our chicken?" he yelled. "Our chicken's gone, Rob! Someone stole our chicken!"

I looked back at the fire. Larry was right, our chicken had disappeared. The willow shafts were still there, but the pieces of chicken were gone. In their place, a small orange flame burned at the end of each shaft. Down amongst the burning branches, scattered in the embers, lay several lumps, burned black. Our tasty morsels. Our stinking roast chicken was . . . .

BAM. BAM. BAM. RATTLE. RATTLE. RATTLE.

A new sound had joined the banging of the hammer. It was the chain. Grandfather was really getting into his role as the judge in the barnyard court. In one hand, he held the logging chain, and in the other, he wielded the ball-peen hammer.

"This is it, kids, your last chance. I've fooled around here long enough. Now it's time to . . . to talk some real turkey!" Grandfather roared. He was really on a roll now. He was grinning again. I recognized that grin—it was the one he always wore when he was about to get someone. Grandfather was about to nail the culprit, I could just feel it. And I knew who it was. I was doomed.

"All of you, into the chicken coop!" he roared. "I want all of you to go into the chicken coop. You take a good look around, and then you come back out and tell me what you see."

I looked at Larry and he looked at me. We didn't need to go into the chicken coop. We knew what was coming.

No one moved.

"Into the chicken coop, I said!" Grandfather roared. With the chain in one hand and the ball-peen hammer in the other, he started around the makeshift table.

Suddenly, everyone was moving. Like scared rats, we all scurried off the bales and through the door. Once on the inside, we all stood very still. We looked around. Then we looked around some more. I was looking around pretty hard, because I, like everyone else, did not want to go back outside and face Grandfather and his ball-peen hammer, or that logging chain. At least, no one wanted to be the first to go back outside. But, even though I looked as hard as I could, all I saw was a bunch of nest boxes. Empty nest boxes. There was not a chicken or an egg in any of them.

"C'mon, git back out here," Grandfather called. "You've looked around enough."

No one moved.

BAM. BAM. BAM. RATTLE. RATTLE. RATTLE.

"C'mon, I said to git out here, or I'm comin' in!" he yelled again. Everyone moved. Slowly, tentatively, we made our way outside and set our little butts back on the row of hay bales.

"What did you see, Girl?" Grandfather asked, pointing the ball-peen hammer at a poor unsuspecting soul.

"N-nothing," came the weak reply.

"Nothin'!" he roared. "That's right. Nothin'. There's nothin' in my chicken coop. There's no chickens. There's no eggs. There's nothin' in there. And do you know why there's nothin' in there?"

I knew why there was nothing in there. Now, it was really time to confess.

"There's nothing in there, 'cause Larry and I stole your chicken," I was about to say.

"There's nothin' in there, because someone has stolen all my nest eggs. I paid good money for them eggs and someone has taken them. They're gone. Every egg from every nest. My chickens are so confused they don't know where to go. There's chickens scattered all over my farm, and they're layin' eggs everywhere: in the barn, in the hayloft. I've even found eggs in the pigpens. But there's no nest eggs. That's why there's nothing in there!" Grandfather roared.

Nest eggs? I never took his dumb old nest eggs, I thought, and a wave of relief spread over me. I looked at Larry, and I was sure I could detect the faintest trace of a smile on his face. Man, was I ever glad that I had been so scared I couldn't open my mouth.

BAM. BAM. BAM.

The hammer slammed the table. Amid the flying dirt and dust and grains of wheat, he hoisted the logging chain above his head. Grandfather was sure mad about losing his nest eggs.

"You've got one more chance," he bellowed, "and if I don't find out who's taken my nest eggs, I . . . I . . ." Grandfather was suddenly lost for words.

We all waited. Grandfather looked around at the kids sitting, petrified, on the bales. He looked at the adults standing around him. He looked at the table. At the ball-peen hammer. Then he looked at the logging chain he was holding in his hand. Now, a real sinister grin spread slowly across his face. He grinned at us kids. He turned and grinned at the adults. Then he threw his arm, the one with the logging chain, high into the air and yelled.

"If someone don't tell me who's stealing my nest eggs, I . . . I'm going to hang your dad!"

That did it. Suddenly everybody's mouth was open. Every kid on every bale was howling. Every kid knew for sure it was his or her dad that was going to be hanged by Grandfather's logging chain.

But not Ma. Ma had seen enough for one day. She had other ideas.

"That's it. That's enough of that foolish talk. Dinner's ready!" she called out loud and clear. With those words, Ma adjourned Grandfather's barnyard court.

"But . . . but Ma. I . . . I'm not finished yet," Grandfather stammered, protesting her decision.

"That's what you think," Ma replied. "C'mon, let's go. Everyone come up to the house, it's time to eat."

Larry and I took one look at each other. Then we bolted off the bales. We charged past Grandfather, who was standing there with the big ball-peen hammer in one hand, a length of logging chain in the other, and his mouth wide open—speechless. We raced towards the house, where the chicken dinner waited. We raced past the house, past the chicken dinner. Out of the driveway we ran, our little legs pumping as fast as pistons. Larry was in the lead as we turned right on the South Road.

There was no way we were hanging around Grandfather's place. Man, if he got that upset about those stupid phony nest eggs, I didn't even want to know what he'd do if he found out about us riding his real-live pigs and killing his egg-laying chicken.

COPPER-WIRE FISHERMAN

I walked to the edge of the road and looked north. I was nervously pacing the driveway, and not-so-patiently waiting. It was a big day in my life. A sunny summer day in June, and I was eagerly awaiting the arrival of Charles, my new friend. He was coming to the Stump Farm, and he and I were going fishing. He was a few years older than I, and certainly not someone I had been fortunate enough to consider a friend. However, in a moment of weakness at school, my bragging had once again provided me with an unexpected opportunity.

I had been telling everyone who would listen about the fish I had been pulling out of Bench Creek. Charles, too, had a reputation as a fisherman, a very good fisherman, and he overheard me talking about having to cram the last fish into my creel. Actually, I didn't really have a creel. I had a war-surplus knapsack that I used for everything—I carried my lunch to school in it; when I hunted grouse, I carried my grouse in it; and when I checked my trapline, I carried my squirrels and weasels in it. But when I was fishing, that old knapsack was a creel.

"Yes siree, boys," I spouted off to the group standing around me, "the last fish I crammed into my creel was a grayling. About a pound, I'd say."

"Say, Bob," interrupted a voice that I had heard only in passing, "how would you like to go fishing with me?"

"Huh?" I mumbled, looking way up to see who had spoken. And there he was, standing a head taller than everyone else, with a big old smile on his face.

"What do you say, Bobby? Let's you and me go fishin' sometime."

My jaw dropped. I looked at Charles and I couldn't believe my ears. Everyone in the schoolyard knew who Charles was. I bet he was the most popular guy in school. He was athletic—he could play any sport, and he was good. He was smart—"at the top of his class," I had heard many a person say. He was rich and important—even I knew this, because his clothes were always a touch above what most of the kids wore. Oh yes, Charles was a very popular, cool dude on the Edson playground. I just couldn't believe my good luck. Charles . . . well, actually, we had always called him Charlie until about a year ago, when he had taken up fly fishing. Having elevated his status in the fishing community, he no longer answered to Charlie. And it was he, Charles himself, who was asking me to go fishing. This was unbelievable. Not in my wildest imagination could I have dreamed of an opportunity like this. It was far too good to pass up.

"You bet!" I replied quickly, before he thought about it and changed his mind. I'd never been fly fishing; in fact, I had never even seen anyone fish with flies. But I loved fishing, and who would have believed that I was going fishing with the number one guy in the school!

"When are we going, Charles?" I hastily added.

Charles stood there silent, thinking, while my friends, all envious, pushed in a little closer. They could not believe their ears either. This was a proud moment, my moment, a moment to treasure. I was the centre of attention. I boldly moved closer to my new friend, beaming with anticipation.

Charles, however, wasn't quite as eager as I. He gave it some careful consideration and thought at length before replying: "How about I come out to your place on Saturday and we go from there?"

"Hey, that's tomorrow!" I shouted excitedly. "You bet!"

"Okay, Bob, see you on Saturday," Charles said, then turned and walked away.

"See you tomorrow, Charles!" I called after him as my friends gathered around me. I just could not believe my good luck. Not only had I been asked to go fishing with Charles, a kid much older than me, but he was coming to my house to boot.

I was so excited that I could hardly sleep that night, and on Saturday morning I was up with the chickens. I raced through my chores, then ran to the road to await the arrival of my new friend.

I saw Charles as he emerged from the draw—first his head, then his shoulders. Finally, he was all there and he sauntered along the road, taking his time. Charles was in no hurry. I couldn't help but marvel at him. He was almost a man and totally in control; that is, until he got opposite Nick-the-Dog-Man's place. The sudden uproar of barking, yapping dogs and the emergence of a number of Nick's puppies, very large puppies, along the side of the road was enough to encourage Charles to change gears. One hand flew to his head and grabbed onto his hat. The other hand clutched his fishing rod. Charles's feet were pounding like pistons as he bolted like a turpentined cat. Nick-the-Dog-Man's puppies just loved it when someone ran. Their barking suddenly changed to loud, ear-piercing, blood-curdling howls, and the chase was on. Poor Charles was kicking up dust as those puppies nipped at his heels. He never stopped running until he was well past Grandfather's place.

I watched until the dogs had returned to Nick-the-Dog-Man's place and Charles had returned to a walk. Then I raced down the road to meet him.

"Hey, Charles," I called, "Dad says don't worry about them dogs, they're only puppies. Dad says they won't bother you as long as you don't run and you leave them alone."

"Yeah, well, you tell your dad not to worry, then," a ruffled Charles panted angrily. "I was leaving them alone, but that didn't stop them from chasing me. Lookit my pants," he said. "Lookit this, they ripped my pants. I hate dogs."

I was more interested in his hat. It sat on the top of his head, all ruffled and scrunched up. Here and there, a colourful fly stuck out of a crinkle in the hatband. The ones I could see looked just like the flies that were on the back of a Sportsman cigarette package. Man, I thought, Charles sure had a lot of flies. Never in my life did I have even one fly for fishing.

"Lookit my pants," he demanded. "They're ruined."

"I know," I said sympathetically. I had seen many a pair of pants that had fallen victim to Nick-the-Dog-Man's puppies, some in even worse shape than Charles's.

"You hafta be real quiet when you walk past Nick-the-Dog-Man's place," I cautioned him. "If you're not, those dogs will charge after you every time."

"How come you didn't warn me about those dogs?" Charles snapped unhappily.

"I'm sorry, Charles," I mumbled apologetically. I could sense that my new friend was not all that impressed with me. "I guess a real friend would have warned you. I'm sorry."

"Don't flatter yourself, kid," Charles snorted, still checking his pants. Poor Charles, right now his clothes didn't look any better than mine.

"You gonna fish with that?" I asked, pointing at the long fishing pole that he was carrying.

"You bet. That's my new fly rod," Charles answered. Suddenly, he forgot about his pants and Nick-the-Dog-Man's dogs. He proudly held the fly rod out in front of him.

"Wow!" I exclaimed, as I reached over to take it. "I never saw a fishin' pole like that before."

Obviously, Charles hadn't held the rod out for me to do anything more than look at. As my hand neared his prized possession, he recoiled as if he had been snake-bitten.

"This ain't a fishin' pole. It's a fly rod," he snapped. "You ever handle a real fly rod?"He jerked the rod away from my hand and held it high, above his head, behind him.

"No," I answered. "I never even seen one before, except maybe in the Simpsons catalogue."

"Well, this rod is brand new and it didn't come out of no catalogue. I ain't gonna let no dumb kid knock the eyes off it before I get to use it," he growled and gave me a dirty look.

I stepped back about three paces. When Charles was sure that I was no longer a threat to his brand new fly rod, the look on his face changed. He lowered his arm and held the fly rod lovingly in front of him. I could only admire it from where I was standing.

"Is that a honest-to-goodness fly reel too?" I asked. Then I leaned forward, being careful not to get too close, for a look at the reel.

"Yeah, that's a honest-to-goodness fly reel too," Charles laughed. "Don't you know anything? What did you think it was, a wheel for a trike or something?"

"I don't know," I muttered. "I guess 'cause I never saw a fly reel up close before, I just thought I'd ask."

"Yeah, well, fly fishin' is for real sportsmen. I don't suppose you know what a real sportsman is. Do you?"

"Sure I do," I answered. "I'm a real sportsman too."

"Sure you are, kid. Where's your fishing rod?" Charles asked.

"I . . . I . . . I don't have one," I mumbled. "I just use an old willow pole."

"Yeah, some sportsman you are," he chuckled. "Well, where's all these fish you've been bragging about?" he demanded. "I can't wait to catch me a whole mess of them. You better not be lying to me."

"I'm not. There's lotsa fish. They're in the creek," I assured him.

"No kidding. How long did it take before you figured that one out?" He chuckled. "Okay, you just point me in the right direction and I'll find it."

"C'mon, I'll show you," I replied.

I looked enviously at the creel he had over his shoulder. It hung just behind his right arm. It would be an easy reach to drop a grayling through the little square hole in the top. Reluctantly, I picked up my knapsack and worked my arms through the straps so that it hung on my back, leaving my hands free for the important aspects of fishing.

"What's that bag for?" Charles asked.

"That's where I'm gonna put my fish," I replied.

"In there?" He recoiled with disgust. "Well, I'm tellin' you, you better not be puttin' any of my fish in that dirty thing," he snorted. Then he pursed his lips, squinted his eyes, and shuddered in disgust.

We left the South Road. We crossed Taylor's field and headed east towards the line of trees in the distance that marked Bench Creek, a small stream that flowed south out of the CNR dam on the west side of Edson. First the stream ran south, then east, then north, almost encircling the Stump Farm.

"I thought we'd start east of the house and work our way upstream," I informed Charles, but he didn't reply. We walked in silence across the field to the edge of the stream.

I had never in my life seen anyone fish with a fly rod before, let alone a brand new fly rod. I was so impressed that I even forgot to cut myself a fishing pole. I watched in awe as Charles very deliberately went through the important steps of setting up his fly rod. He checked every eyelet. Then he checked the reel, then the line. Finally, he fed the line through the eyes, right to the end of the fly rod. Once the rod, reel, and line were assembled to his satisfaction, he took his hat from his head to study the assortment of flies stuck in the hatband. Flies that were covered with little feathers, hair, and coloured thread.

"So, there's a bunch of grayling in here," Charles said, speaking to himself.

"Mostly," I replied, "but we do catch the odd jack as well."

"Yeah, well, I don't want any stinking, slimy old jacks," Charles stated emphatically. "Tell me, what kind of flies are the grayling hitting right now?"

"I don't know," I replied, shrugging my shoulders. "Live ones, I guess." Charles gave me a very disgusted look.

"See this hook?" he said, when he had finally removed one from his hat. "This is a Royal Coachman.

It's a real grayling killer. I knock 'em dead with this one."

"Can I see it?" I asked. I wanted to see what a real grayling killer looked like, so I took a step closer. A swift, snarly glance from Charles told me that I was once again infringing on forbidden territory. I looked at the Royal Coachman from a distance while Charles tied it to the end of the line.

"There's a really good hole just ahead," I said and pointed upstream. I sort of thought that we'd follow the trail and walk around the clump of willows, but not so. Charles led and I followed. We approached the creek very slowly, for the spot where Charles chose to make his entrance was right through the willow patch. Clutching his brand new fly rod and the line tightly in one hand, he barged forward.

He did his best to fend off the tangle of willow branches with his free hand, but there were just too many. Charles cursed as one after another, errant branches slapped him in the face and even picked the hat neatly off his head. I followed along behind at a safe distance, being careful not to get too close to the brand new fly rod. Finally, Charles plowed his way through to the clearing.

"This is it. It's a really good spot," I called up to Charles. "I always see fish in this hole."

"Shhh. Shut up, stupid," Charles growled at me. "What're you trying to do, scare my fish?"

Charles crouched down; then he tiptoed into the clearing. He slowly lifted his head and peered over the bank into the water. Instantly, he flapped his arm up and down, motioning me to squat down.

"I found them. There's a beaut in here," he whispered. "I can see him real plain. He's right out in the middle, just waiting for my hook. You just stay still and be sure you don't scare him. Now watch yourself, because I'm gonna cast."

Charles slowly raised the tip of his rod out over the water and let the Royal Coachman and the line drop free. The hook, with its coloured feathers, dangled at the edge of the stream, several feet over the surface of the water.

"That's too high," I offered in a very low voice. From my vantage point, still squatting in the willows behind Charles, I couldn't see the water or the grayling.

"Charles," I called a little louder, "your hook's too high. Let out a little more line and cast again."

"I'm gonna drop this fly on the water just above his head," Charles snorted as he turned and gave me a contemptuous look. He was not very impressed with me. I hunkered down a little lower and stayed real quiet.

Very slowly, Charles lifted his arm, and the tip of the rod rose. As smooth as a well-oiled machine, he pulled his arm back and up. The Royal Coachman fly zipped up away from the water. *Zzzzzz,* it buzzed as it cut through the air, following the line. Up it flew, up and back, over our heads. I ducked a little lower. It was like watching poetry in motion, as Charles' arm moved back, then forward. Suddenly, the Royal Coachman fly changed direction and was now *zzzzzz*ipping back towards the water. Charles brought his arm back again, then forward. He repeated this graceful exercise several times, and each time more line came out and the Royal Coachman was flying in ever greater arcs. Yes, I thought, Charles was indeed a fly fisherman. Then, with a slight flick of his wrist, Charles aimed that Royal Coachman at the spot on the water just above the grayling's head.

TWANG. I was so surprised at the sudden change of events that I jumped up. Charles' line sang out as it went tight. Taut as a fiddle string it was. Charles's brand new fly rod sprang into action. It bent like Hiawatha's bow, and the tip danced around in the air.

Charles cursed.

"Hey, Charlie," I shouted excitedly, "you caught— "

But Charles cut me off with a wicked glare. Then he cursed some more. For it was not that beaut of a grayling on the end of his line. Charles's brand new fly rod was bent backwards, and the Royal Coachman fly was firmly embedded in a willow branch high above my head. Charles tugged on the brand new fly rod, and the willow branch tugged right back. The Royal Coachman fly held fast.

Once more, I hunkered down in the willows and watched the master at work, as he carefully freed the hook. Then he took a small carborundum stone and carefully touched up the hook. Without a word, he promptly repeated the cast. Casting a fly on the banks of Bench Creek was not an easy task, even for an experienced fisherman like Charles.

A number of futile attempts and several well-hooked willows later, Charles decided that a change in tactics was required. Instead of trying to cast the fly, Charles let the Royal Coachman dangle over the creek. Then, with a flick of his wrist, he deftly flicked the hook upstream and allowed the fly to float, on the surface, over the grayling. While this attempt did not yield any more willows, it was no more successful with the grayling.

"Grayling aren't hitting Royal Coachman on the surface right now," Charles informed me. "I'm gonna sink it right in front of his nose." He dug into his pockets and produced a small ball of lead shot, which he attached to the line. Then he flicked the Royal Coachman and the lead shot upstream.

PLOP. It sounded as if Charles had tossed a boulder into the water.

From my vantage point in the willows behind Charles, I was really in the dark. I couldn't see a thing. I moved forward, walked way around him, and came in to the edge of the stream up ahead of him. Man, I thought as I looked into the water, Charles was right. There was a grayling, and it really was a beaut. I watched as the weighted line pulled the Royal Coachman down into the water towards the big grayling.

As the hook passed by in front of its nose, the grayling moved aside to let it pass.

"He's interested now," Charles whispered excitedly over his shoulder to where I had originally been crouching. "He almost took it that time. You watch, I'll get him now." Charles pulled the hook, line, and sinker out of the water and once more flicked it upstream.

"He's mine. I've got his attention now." Once more, the hook passed within inches of the grayling, and once more, with a flick of its tail the grayling moved to one side.

Now, I don't mind admitting that seeing this fish in one of my favourite fishing holes was just a little more than I could take. Quickly, I moved back into the willows and selected myself a nice, long, slender willow that had very few little limbs on it. With one swipe of my jackknife, I cut it down and quickly knocked off the few limbs and the tip. From my knapsack, I retrieved an old roll of copper wire. I twisted a good length off the roll and made a little eye on one end. The other end I fed through the eye to form a small loop, then I twisted it tightly onto the tip of the willow. My new fishing pole, much newer than Charles's, albeit not nearly as elaborate, was now ready.

"What do you think you're doing?" Charles demanded, almost yelling at me. He had been so intent on watching the Royal Coachman drift by that grayling that he hadn't even see me move up to the stream bank ahead of him. But I sure had his attention when he realized I had dipped the tip of my brand new fishing pole into the water.

"I'm going to catch me that fish," I replied as Charles's Royal Coachman floated past the grayling for the umpteenth time.

"With that stick? I don't think so!" He laughed. "I've never seen anything so stupid in my life. Anyway, it's way too short."

"No it's not. I catch fish like this all the time," I replied.

"Sure you do," he said, killing himself laughing.

With my left hand, I grabbed hold of a small clump of willows growing on the bank. Then, I leaned way out over the water. With my fishing pole clutched in my right hand, I slowly reached out and lowered the tip of the pole deeper into the water in front of the grayling. Slowly, the loop of copper wire descended. When I was satisfied that the loop was right in front of the grayling, I let the current take the pole and the copper-wire loop back. The grayling did not move away from the wire loop as it had from the Royal Coachman. Slowly the loop passed round its head. When it was around the gills, I yanked the willow pole up, real fast. Instantly, I could feel the grayling struggling on the end of the pole. In one motion, almost as smooth as Charles' cast, I flipped the pole, copper wire, and wildly thrashing grayling up into the air. The whole works sailed over my head and landed in the grass behind the willows. I raced back to where the fish was flopping on the ground and grabbed it with both hands. I carefully removed the wire loop from its gills, and I held my prize high for my new friend to admire.

"I caught him, Charles," I sang out. "I caught him. Isn't he a beaut?" Now, an Arctic grayling has a beautifully coloured large dorsal fin, and I stretched it out for Charles to admire. He just stood there like he was stunned. His mouth hung open and he stared at me. Aha, I thought, Charles can't believe what a good fisherman I am.

"You . . . you . . . you can't do that!" he yelled when he was finally able to speak. He was stammering and stuttering, and his eyes were bulging out. Charles really couldn't believe what he had just witnessed.

"Sure I can," I assured him. "Here, I'll show you." I slipped the grayling into my creel, my old army-surplus knapsack, and raced back up to the edge of the stream. I had learned long ago that there was usually more than one grayling in this hole. I searched the pool, and worked my way back to the ripples at the back end of the pool. Sure enough, there in the faster-flowing water, I could see another grayling. The head and eye just seemed to shimmer in the ripples. Once again, I leaned forward and dipped the end of the willow pole into the water. The copper wire and the end of the willow pole danced in the ripples. I figured that catching a grayling in the ripples, where it was harder to follow the dancing snare, was sure to impress Charles.

"What . . . what do you think you're doing now?" asked a horrified Charles.

"I'm gonna catch me another fish," I answered triumphantly, for at that very moment the copper loop slipped around another set of gills, and as quickly and smoothly as with that beaut of a grayling, I yanked a second grayling from the waters of Bench Creek.

"That's illegal," howled my mortified friend.

"No it's not," I answered as I deposited the second fish into my creel. "It's a fish."

"No . . . no . . . no!" he wailed. "That's poaching! It's illegal! You can't do that!"

"Why not?" I asked, as the fish continued to flop

around on the inside of the knapsack.

"Because . . . because you can go to jail for snaring fish, that's why. It's illegal!"

"No it's not," I replied and laughed. "Out here we call this fishin', and I do it all the time."

"Well . . . well, it's not fishing to me," he stammered. "No way, that's not fishing," he snorted. Then he tucked his brand new fly rod under his arm and plowed his way back through the willows. Charles was still blowing off steam as he started back across Taylor's field.

Then it hit me – my new friend was leaving. He was going home. As I watched him stomping through the grass, I wondered what I had done to insult him.

"Hey, Charles, c'mon back!" I called after him, pleading with him not to leave. "C'mon, Charles . . . Charles, c'mon . . . there's another fish here, I can see it. Its just in the ripples. Please, Charles, c'mon back. Charles, I'll let you catch the next fish. I promise."

But Charles was having nothing more to do with me or my method of fishing.

"Charles!" I yelled one more time. "Don't forget about Nick-the-Dog-Man's puppies!"

THE FRIENDLY BANK TELLER

For as long as I could remember, Dad had worked in the bush camps. Dad's bags—well, actually, *a* bag, an old beat-up cardboard suitcase tied together with binder twine—was always packed long before the snow flew and the ground froze. Regular as clockwork, as soon as the trucks could safely cross the muskegs, Dad would leave for the camps. Except for a couple of days at Christmas, he would spend the winter in the bush, away from his family.

Being a catskinner in the bush camps meant that he rarely, if ever, saw the inside of many of the businesses in Edson. In particular, I doubt that he had ever seen the inside of the Imperial Bank. Consequently, the business of running the household and looking after the family's needs was left in Mom's very capable hands. If a meeting with the local banker was needed, it was Mom who met with him. If Dad's signature was required, Mom would simply bring the document home and take whatever steps were necessary to finalize it. Yes, as a rule Mom handled all of the family's business affairs; she was the family business manager.

Every once in a while, circumstances changed. And with change came exceptions to the rule.

It was late on a Thursday night, the last Thursday before Christmas, when a major change occurred. There was a noise at the door. Then, suddenly, the door flew open and a beat-up old cardboard suitcase, tied with binder twine, was pushed in. It was followed quickly by none other than Dad. Christmas wasn't until Monday and he wasn't due home for at least two more days. It was an unexpected pleasure. An extended weekend. Dad was home for the holidays.

"Yea, Dad's home!" we all sang out and raced to the door to greet him. Well, we all raced to the door except Mom. She just sat at the table. She looked as if she had seen a ghost.

"What's wrong, Bob?" were Mom's first words of greeting.

"Nothing," Dad replied as kids swarmed around him. I grabbed his old beat-up suitcase and dragged it away from the door.

"Are you okay? You're not sick, are you? Did you get hurt?" The questions came rapid-fire, one after the other, before Dad even had time to answer, let alone take his coat off.

"I'm fine, Florence," he replied.

"Did the mill close down? Do you still have a job?"

It was not like Dad to leave the camp early. Not quite accepting the fact that he was home Mom had not been able to drag herself away from the kitchen table. She was worried.

"Everything's just fine and dandy," Dad replied happily. "They just shut down a day early for Christmas, and I was able to hitch a ride out tonight, so here I am."

"Yea!" we all cheered. Mom didn't cheer. She knew it wasn't normal for Dad to take extra days off. She knew the consequences only too well—the most serious, of course, being money. Dad only got paid for the days he worked. An extra day at Christmas might be great from the kids' point of view, but it meant a smaller paycheque at the end of the month. Mom, the business manager, was concerned, and with good reason. I think she was already figuring what this day would cost us. Somewhere down the line, she would have to make adjustments. There would be a little less.

"You're sure you're all right? There's nothing wrong?" Mom asked again.

"You betcha I'm all right," Dad sang out. He wasn't nearly as worried as Mom was. But then, Dad had never had to face the man at the grocery store and beg for more credit, nor had he ever faced the banker.

"I was thinking that Bob and I could do a little shopping tomorrow," he continued.

Dad shopping? We all stopped and looked at him. This was really a surprise, because for as long as I could remember, Dad had never gone shopping. Shopping was the domain of the business manager, Mom.

"You're going to do a little *what?"* Mom asked.

"Shopping," Dad chuckled. "I thought maybe Bob and I could check out a couple of stores. We might even drop in at the Beanery. We can chinwag with some of the boys and have us a cup of coffee."

I whistled. "Oh yeah! Chinwaggin' and coffee with Dad and the boys at the Beanery. That sounds pretty darned good if you ask me."

Mom sat there thinking about what Dad had said. Then she looked at me and shook her head.

"I don't see how that'll work," Mom stated. "You know Bobby has school tomorrow?"

"I don't think it will hurt him to miss one day," Dad replied. "I reckon it might even do him some good. I can't see any harm in a boy spending a day with his father. You know, he's almost a man now."

"Oh yes, I know all right. He reminds me of it every chance he gets. Tell me, what are you going to use for money?" Mom asked. "There isn't a cent in the house."

"Don't you worry your pretty little head none about that," Dad chuckled confidently. Then he patted his hip pocket and smiled. "I got my paycheque right here in my wallet."

"Wow!" I exclaimed. "You mean you got a real cheque, Dad?" I had never seen a real paycheque before. In the summer, when Dad did odd jobs in town, he always got paid in cash. I remember Mom often looking sadly at the few dollar and coins lying on the table. But a few dollars were better than no dollars at all. And now I would get to go to town with Dad and watch him cash a real cheque.

Mom suddenly got a sick look on her face.

"No, Bob, you can't do that. I can see a couple of problems," Mom replied. I got the feeling that she was not too keen on Dad going to town. There was silence around the table as we all considered what the problems might be. It beat me, I couldn't think of a single one. Then Mom finally spoke again.

"You know your cheque is spoken for," Mom cautioned. Mom was dead serious now. "There's never enough money to pay the bank loan and the grocery bill. We . . . we just don't have enough money to go around. Maybe I should take your cheque into town and settle up some of our accounts. Then . . . then if there's anything left, you and Bobby can—"

"You know, Florence," Dad said, cutting her short, "after I cash my cheque, I think I can pay those bills. Then, Bob and I can mosey around a little before we get that cup of coffee." That comment should have ended the conversation, but it did not. It did little to ease the mind of the business manager, who had to get the last word in.

"I don't think that's such a good idea, Bob. I think I should be with you when you two go to the bank."

"It'll be okay," Dad assured her. "Me and Bob will do just fine."

This sounded great to me. It was a rare opportunity. I wouldn't have to go to school. I'd get to spend time with Dad, and for the first time in my life, I'd get to go into the bank. This was an opportunity I didn't want to miss. I was so excited, I could hardly sleep that night.

There were mixed emotions in our house the next

morning. Dad was whistling and singing. He had taken over Mom's cookstove and whipped up a hefty pile of pancakes. Dad was a right jolly fellow this morning. I was happy as a lark. I wolfed down more than my share of pancakes, revelling in Dad's good spirits. Mom, however, did not share Dad's carefree mood. She looked worried.

"Well, as long as you insist on going into town without me, I might as well get you to run a couple of errands for me," Mom sighed. She had resigned herself to the idea of Dad and me moseying around town for the day.

"You betcha," Dad chuckled. "I think we can handle that. What do you think, Bob?" Man, but Dad was in a good mood.

"You betcha!" I yodelled happily. "You just name it, Mom. Me and Dad'll do it."

"I need a few things from the grocery store."

"What do you say, Bob? Do you think we can handle a couple of things from the grocery store?" Dad asked, and smiled.

"I don't think so," I replied.

"Oh, I think we can. What kind of things do you need, Florence?" Dad asked.

"Here, I've made a list for you," Mom said, handing Dad a piece of paper. It was a large piece of brown paper, probably torn from a bag.

"You . . . you want me to get all this?" Dad asked. The smile was fading. He was staring at all the words scribbled on the paper.

"When you get into town, just give the order to Mr.

Goldsmith. He'll fill it and you can pick it up when you're ready to come home."

"I guess we're gonna hafta take the kids' sleigh," Dad mumbled.

"We can't go to the grocery store," I butted in, adding my two cents' worth. "The last time I was there, Mr. Goldsmith said he was very sorry, he knew times were tough, but before he could extend any more credit, we'd have to pay our bill. He said he had bills to pay and a family to feed, too."

"That won't be a problem now," Mom stated. "Your father has it all worked out. When he cashes his paycheque, he can make the loan payment, and then you can go and pay Mr. Goldsmith and leave the order with him."

"I think we can handle that all right," Dad chuckled. "Go fetch the sleigh, Bob. It's time to get goin'."

"Not so fast," Mom said. "Since you're going to town, you might as well stop by the garage and pick up the batteries for the radio."

"Pick up the batteries," Dad sort of mumbled. The smile had disappeared from his face.

"That's right. As long as you're going into town anyway, you might just as well pick up the batteries. It's either that, or we won't be able to listen to the radio over Christmas. And they always have such beautiful music on at this time of the year. I just love to listen to the Christmas carols." Mom's voice was suddenly soft and relaxed. She got that faraway look in her eye.

"You know, Florence, I can always play the guitar," Dad said. "The kids like to sing along." Dad didn't really want to pick up the radio batteries, and I didn't blame him. Our radio ran on two batteries, one an A battery and the other a B battery. Those suckers were huge and they were heavy. They were the size of car batteries. In fact, I think they were really meant to be used in cars—or more likely in trucks, they were that big. They were always losing their power, and every time they ran down, they had to be taken into town and recharged at the garage.

"You can still play the guitar," Mom replied. "And the kids can have their singsong, but at Christmas it is nice to be able to listen to the music on the radio."

"Well, okay," Dad said weakly. "I hadn't planned on it, but I suppose I can get the batteries."

"I can pull the batteries on the sleigh, Dad," I quickly volunteered. I didn't want a little thing like the radio batteries keeping me from moseying around town and stopping in at the Beanery with Dad.

"Gee willikers," Dad mumbled, but he mumbled it very quietly. "I don't think I'll get the batteries and the groceries all on the sleigh."

"Then you'll just have to do like I do, and carry some of it," Mom stated.

Finally Dad and I left the house, walking. Well, Dad walked while I strutted proudly and pulled the sleigh. But walking or strutting, I stuck to Dad like glue. We walked to the Imperial Bank, which was located at the corner of 5th and Main.

"How come Mom didn't want us to go to town and mosey around and have coffee with the boys?" I asked.

"I don't rightly know," Dad replied. "It might be

because she's home alone with you kids all winter and is used to doing everything herself."

"Yeah, well, we'll sure show her. She probably thinks we can't do it, huh, Dad?"

We marched through the door into the bank. Dad stopped for a second or two and looked around. There were two wickets. Both had lineups. He picked one and stepped to the end of the line, waiting his turn. I stood beside him, watching the people ahead of us.

"Wow, Dad, lookit that!" I blurted out and pointed. A man had just left the wicket. He paused for a minute, almost in front of me, while he thumbed through a fistful of bills. There were bills of every colour. Except for the green ones, I had never seen any of the bills before. That one man had more money than I had ever seen in my whole life.

"Don't point, Bob," Dad replied. He reached out and pushed my arm down. "It's not polite." Dad just ignored the man and the wad of money he carried.

"Holy cow!" I exclaimed. "Dad, did you ever see so much money in your life?"

Being on the inside of a bank was really exciting. I was bug-eyed in awe, and I couldn't wait for Dad to get his fistful of money. I watched the man stuff the wad into his pocket. Then he put his hands into his pockets and shuffled away. I never took my eyes off him until he disappeared out the door.

"Are you gonna get that much money too, Dad?" I asked. Just then, Dad nudged me.

"Let's go, Bob. It's our turn," Dad said, jarring me back to reality. I stepped right smart-like, alongside

Dad, up to the counter like I owned the place. And I knew I'd own the place, just as soon as Dad got his wad of money. I watched his every move. I noticed how he slipped his thumb and index finger into his hip pocket and pulled out his wallet.

"Well hello, stranger!" the friendly bank teller greeted him. She looked surprised. Then she looked around past him, as if looking for someone else.

"Oh, hello," Dad replied as he carefully opened his worn old wallet. Then he took out his paycheque.

"Oh . . . oh hi, Bobby," she said, acknowledging me as an afterthought. "How come you're not in school today?"

"I come with Dad, to help him carry all his money," I blurted out. "An' . . . an' we're going to the Beanery to have a cuppa coffee," I quickly added.

"I see. And to what do we owe this honour, Bob?" She looked through her wicket, smiling at Dad.

"Oh, I just came in to cash my paycheque," Dad replied. I watched proudly as he slid his paycheque under the wicket to the friendly bank teller.

"Where's Florence?" asked the teller as she flipped the cheque over and looked at the back. She had a curious look on her face.

"Oh, she's at home, gettin' ready for Christmas," Dad replied.

"But your cheque's not signed, Bob. It has to be signed before I can cash it." She pushed Dad's paycheque back under the wicket.

"Oh . . . Oh, is that so? Well, I guess I better sign it, then," Dad chuckled. She looked at him for a second, and then reluctantly handed him her pen. He carefully examined the front of the cheque.

"How come you gotta sign your cheque, Dad?" I asked.

"I don't know," he replied and shrugged his shoulders. "It must be something new. I don't recall having to sign them in the past."

"You can just sign it anywhere on the back, Bob," she informed him.

"All rightee," Dad replied hesitantly. He turned it over and looked at the back of the cheque, a blank piece of paper.

"Just sign your name anywhere," said the teller. I pushed in as close as I could get and watched Dad as he signed his paycheque.

"When did you get back into town, Bob?" she asked, obviously much more interested in talking than in cashing his cheque.

"Last night," Dad replied. Very deliberately, he signed his name, then carefully looked it over before pushing the cheque back under the wicket.

"You're home early this year. How long are you in town for this time?"

"Just for Christmas. Then I have to go back to camp," he replied.

"Isn't that good. I'll bet Florence was surprised and happy to see you." She smiled.

"Surprised!" The words just sort of jumped out of my mouth. Lady, I thought, you don't know the half of it.

"Are you and Florence going to get a chance to come

by the house for a little cheer?" she asked.

"That sounds good, but I'm not sure what Florence has planned," Dad replied. "I'll mention it to her when I get home."

Hurry up and cash the cheque, I urged them silently. I was anxious to see Dad's wad of money and to get out of the bank so Dad and I could mosey around some. I could already taste the pop I was going to get when we stopped at the Beanery.

"Well, we certainly hope we'll get a chance to see you before you have to go back to camp," she said.

Then she picked up Dad's paycheque. She looked at the face of the cheque. She turned it over and looked at his signature on the back. The smile was gone. The small talk was over. We were onto the serious business of banking. This was the part I was waiting for. Dad was going to get his wad of money.

"One moment, please, Mr. Adams," she said. I couldn't believe it when she left her wicket. She turned and walked away, with Dad's paycheque.

"Hey, Dad! She took your cheque and she didn't give you any money!" I blurted out, surprised at this turn of events. I heard several people behind us chuckle.

"It's okay," Dad replied calmly. "She'll be right back."

As usual, he was right. To me, it seemed like she was gone forever, but in only a few minutes, that friendly bank teller returned with a smile on her face. She made sure she took up her place at the wicket before she spoke.

"I'm sorry, Mr. Adams," said the teller. I noticed that when she talked bank business, Dad was no longer "Bob", he was "Mr. Adams". Although she wore a smile, she had lost much of the friendliness she had shown when we first walked up to her cage. Now she was all business.

"I'm sorry, but I can't cash this cheque."

"What!" I blurted out. I couldn't believe my ears. I quickly looked up at Dad. Obviously, he couldn't believe his ears either. He just stood there with his mouth open. Unable to say a word. He looked as if he had just been kicked by a horse.

"Oh" was the only word that escaped from his lips for the longest time.

Oh no, I thought, there goes our day moseying around. There goes coffee with the boys down at the Beanery.

"Why not? Is there something wrong with the cheque?" he asked, sounding very concerned.

"Oh no, there's nothing wrong with the cheque. It's fine." She was struggling to keep the smile on her face.

"I don't understand, then. Why can't you cash it?" he asked again, with a look of complete bewilderment on his face.

"Well," she sighed, "Bank policy states that I have to verify your signature with the one we have on file before I can cash any cheque." Dad and I both watched as she flipped the cheque over and showed us the back, where Dad had signed.

"You see, Mr. Adams, before I can cash your cheque, it has to have the proper signature on the back," she stated. "And this cheque does not have the proper signature on it."

"But . . . but you just watched me sign it," Dad stammered. "And . . . and you know me. You know I'm Bob Adams, don't you?" he asked, not believing what was happening to him.

"Of course I know you, Mr. Adams," she shot back, resenting the fact that she should be asked such a question.

"Is this cheque not made out to me, Bob Adams?" he inquired, as he looked at the front of the cheque.

"It certainly is," she replied with a cold stare.

"And you saw me stand right here and sign it?" Dad said. "I don't understand where the problem is."

"I'm sorry, Mr. Adams, but this isn't your signature. I just checked the sample, and this is not the signature we have on file for you. I can't accept this cheque with this signature."

"But it's the only signature I've got," Dad protested. "You watched me sign my cheque. What do you want me to do?"

"You have to have the correct signature before I can cash your cheque, Mr. Adams," she said firmly. "There's nothing I can do about it. It's Bank policy."

"But Florence always cashes my cheques," Dad replied. "She doesn't have any trouble – at least not that I know of. Does she?"

"No, she doesn't," said the teller. "That's because Florence always obtains the proper signature before she comes in."

"What's the matter, Dad?" I asked. "Aren't we gonna get any money?"

"It doesn't look like it," he replied, completely bewildered.

"What are we gonna do now?" I asked.

"I guess we're gonna hafta go back home and talk to your mother," he replied unhappily.

At that point, I bet Dad was thinking the same thing as I was. It wasn't that Mom didn't want us to spend the day together. Mom didn't want Dad taking his cheque to the bank. At least not before it had the *proper* signature on it. Suddenly, I had a pretty good idea why Dad couldn't cash his own cheque.

"You bring your cheque back to me as soon as you've got the proper signature on it, Mr. Adams," she said very officiously. Then she paused, and once more her face lit up.

"Oh, and say hi to Florence for me. Now, Bob, don't you forget to tell her that we'll be expecting to see you all sometime this weekend," sang the friendly bank teller. "Bye now. See you later."

Dad never said a word. He wasn't smiling. Bob wasn't impressed. Neither was Mr. Adams.

DEATHLY ILL

Oh man, but I ached. My throat was so dry, I could hardly swallow. My head was throbbing. My teeth hurt. Every hair on my body felt like a needle being driven into my skin. There was no doubt that I was ill, deathly ill.

I made a valiant attempt to get out of bed. Slowly, I crawled out from under the covers and inched my legs over the side of the bed. My feet dropped to the floor, two lifeless chunks of flesh and bone, and splatted on the linoleum. Immediately, shivers rippled up my legs and across my pain-racked body. No sooner had my feet hit the floor when goosebumps the size of pine cones jumped out all over my skin. As quickly as I could, I dragged my poor, aching body back in under the covers.

"C'mon, Bobby," Mom called. "This is the last time I'm calling you. If you don't get a move on, you're going to be late for school."

I ignored Mom—not a wise thing to do, but I knew I was going to die anyway, so death might just as well come at Mom's hands as from some unknown disease.

"Bobby! You get yourself out of that bed right now!" Mom demanded sharply. "I told you, I'm not calling you again."

I pulled the covers over my head. If I was going to die, I would die in my bed.

"Bobby, what's the matter with you?" Mom asked. Her voice, very near now, cut through the covers. Mom was no longer calling from the kitchen. Mom was in my bedroom, standing over my bed, and she was not happy.

"I'm dying," I croaked.

"Let me see," she said as she yanked the covers off.

This time, it was the blast of cold air, the frigid air of a winter night, that sent another round of shivers rippling over my body. Another crop of pine-cone-sized goosebumps burst out on my skin. My teeth began to chatter uncontrollably.

Then Mom laid her ice-cold hand on my forehead. I let out a loud gasp, and grabbed for the covers. I pulled them over me, right up to my eyes. I would have pulled them higher, but Mom's hand was still on my forehead.

"You don't seem to be that sick," she snorted. "You don't have a fever."

"I do. I . . . I'm burning up," I protested. "I'm . . . I'm dying."

"I don't think you're that sick," Mom replied. "I'm sure you'll feel better once you get up and start moving around."

Who was Mom kidding? It was the middle of January. It was freezing outside and almost as cold inside. It was going to be like every other winter day on the Stump Farm. Cold, cold and miserable. I stayed where I was, lying in bed. Shivering and dying. There was no way I was well enough to go to school.

"I can't go to school, Mom. I'm dying," I repeated.

"I suppose you could be getting the measles. Lord alone knows they're going around again." She sighed. "What am I going to do now? I'm supposed to go to town to see the doctor this morning."

"It's okay. You go to town, Mom. I'll be all right," I croaked. "I'm the man of the house now, I can take care of myself."

Mom left the room and returned with a big jar of Vicks. She rubbed my chest and throat, then tucked me in under the blanket.

"I hate to leave you home alone when you're sick," Mom said. "Are you sure you don't feel like getting up?"

"You go ahead and go to town," I squeaked. "I'll be okay." She left the room again and soon returned with a towel. Off went the sheets and up came my pyjama top. Before the goosebumps had time to sprout, she plunked that towel on my chest. It was a towel that she had put in the oven to warm up and drive the sickness from my body.

"Whoa!" I bellowed. "That's hot." Instinctively, I started to sit up.

"That's just the way it's supposed to be," Mom replied. She pushed me back and pulled the pyjama top down and the covers up. Before I had a chance to blink, she had plastered a big gob of Vicks under my nose. In a matter of seconds, I was roasting, and sweating like a hog.

Mom sure knew how to cure whatever ailed a person.

I heard the shuffling at the door as my brother and sisters, left for school. They would get a ride with Ted Sliva, the milkman and our unofficial school-bus driver. Long before the days of school buses, Ted, as he did on many a school morning, would pick us up and take us into Edson. We were always grateful for the ride, although on a winter morning, sitting on the back of that uncovered truck, it was awfully cold. I was happy to be in bed.

After everyone left for school, for some reason, I started to feel much better. I sure surprised Mom when I walked out into the kitchen to keep her company. She surprised me when she marched me back into the bedroom and tucked me in, then thrust another gob of Vicks up my nose and another hot towel under my pyjama top. Mom was going to roast anything and everything out of me. I guess she figured that if I was going to die, I should do it in my bedroom, not in her kitchen.

It was a trying time for Mom. She was torn between going to town or staying home with me. I could tell that she was worried. She made several trips into the bedroom. Each time, she would check my temperature by putting her hand on my forehead, and then she would check my belly for spots. She looked relieved when my temperature didn't seem to be rising and there were no spots, but that didn't stop the Vicks and the hot towels. A fresh dose of each came with every visit.

Finally, it was decision time. Mom could either start walking into town, to get to her appointment on time, or she could stay home and nurse me.

"You go ahead and go into town, Mom," I squeaked. "I'll be okay, I promise."

Mom was not fully convinced that I would be okay, but she finally decided that she must go. I thought I would start recovering as soon as I could get away from all the Vicks and the hot towels.

"I want you to stay in bed while I'm gone," Mom said sternly, "and I want you to keep the curtains drawn. If you're getting the measles, you have to stay in a dark room or else you'll ruin your eyes."

"I know, Mom," I replied meekly. "I'll stay in bed. I promise."

I could see the sadness in her eyes when she checked in on me for the last time. She carefully tucked one more hot towel under my pyjamas and one more gob of Vicks up my nose, then she turned and walked out of the room. I heard her stoking the stove, putting another log in the firebox. Then the door creaked, and I shivered again at the thought of the cold air streaming in. Mom was walking into town. I was alone.

It seemed as if Mom had been gone for a long time. I was restless; I tossed and turned and I fussed around in my bed. It was no fun being sick in bed, and home alone to boot. I rolled over, and I noticed there was a bright light coming through the bedroom door, and my bedroom was—well, it seemed brighter than usual for a winter day. In fact, it seemed to be very nice and bright and . . . warm. Could this be?

I bounced out of bed and charged into the kitchen to check on the source of the light. I looked out the kitchen window into a bright, sunny winter's day. Then I noticed that Mom hadn't really been gone that long—she hadn't even got to the gate yet. I stepped back away from the window as she reached the South Road and turned left, heading north towards Edson.

Oh, but it was a bright, sunny day out there! Rays of sunshine burst into the kitchen, melting Jack Frost's painting on the windowpanes. Little rivulets flowed down the windows and onto the sills. I could hear the water gurgling as it ran down the roof. It flowed over the icicles that hung like huge crystal fangs from the eaves. I could hear the *plunk, plonk, plink* of the water dripping off the icicles. Outside, I saw the boughs of the spruce and pine trees gently swaying. There was a light breeze. A warm breeze.

"Hot dog!" I sang out. "There's a chinook blowing." This was certainly not a day to be wasted inside.

Suddenly, I felt much better. Mom's hot towels and Vicks had done the trick. I felt my forehead. Mom was right, I didn't have much of a fever after all. No, the more I thought about it, the more I knew I didn't have a fever. In fact, I knew the reason why I hadn't felt good that morning.

It had all started yesterday, at school. There had been an arithmetic quiz, with a little bit of a trick to it. I had just begun to work on the first question when know-it-all Margaret let out an ear-shattering screech.

"I know what the trick is!" she squealed joyfully when the last numbers of the quiz had been written on the blackboard.

I looked at the first question again, and worked harder to figure out the answer. I looked at Margaret, sitting there with her hands folded on her desk. She had the smuggest look on her face. I hate Margaret, I muttered to myself. Then I gritted my teeth and worked on the second question, and the third. I worked like a slave over every one of those questions. I don't know what Margaret was so happy about, I muttered to myself. Every question was just as hard as the last. I couldn't find the trick.

"I got a hundred percent," Margaret boasted triumphantly after the teacher had written the answer under each of the questions.

"So what?" I grumbled. "So did everyone else." Actually, I had got half of them wrong. How was I to know that each question had the same answer? What a stupid trick.

But enough about the quiz; that was yesterday and this was today. And what a beautiful day it was! I knew exactly what a day like this meant. Out in the forest the squirrels would be scurrying through the trees, chattering and eating pine cones. Ah, yes, this was the perfect day for hunting squirrels on my trapline.

I wasted little time getting into my squirrel-hunting duds. I grabbed Grandfather's .22, the one with the shaved-down stock. It was nice and light, easy to pack in the bush. It was the best squirrel-hunting gun in the whole world. As I walked out to greet the day, I grabbed my knapsack and slung it over my back. The first stop on my trapline would be a clump of spruce trees over on Taylor's farm.

I followed the trail south and east from the house until I came to the South Road. I stopped and listened, to check whether there were any vehicles coming, before I walked out onto the South Road. To the north, I could still see Mom, walking towards Edson. I crossed the South Road and, following my well-worn trail through the snow, I walked over a small hill, through a stand of pine and willows where we picked blueberries every fall. As I entered the stand of spruce trees, a flutter of wings erupted behind me. I whirled around, just in time to see a partridge fly up and land on the branches of a spruce tree. It perched there, gawking down at me—but not for long. Not only was Grandfather's trusty .22 a good squirrel gun, it was also a real good partridge gun. In a second, that bird was mine. I picked the eye right out of the little sucker. Boy, I thought, will Mom ever be surprised when she sees the little beauty that I got for supper.

As I picked up the partridge, a squirrel chattered. I left the trail, plucking our supper, and walked in the direction of his call. It was just as I'd imagined it. On such a beautiful day, that squirrel was calling me. Before long, I found the telltale sign of a squirrel – fresh-chewed pine cones scattered on the snow under a tall pine tree. Scanning the branches carefully, I spotted the little devil. He was way up near the top of the tree, sitting quiet as a mouse. Again I used Grandfather's .22. Another shot, right in the eye. Man, was I good!

"I bet I could hit the eye of a fly at 200 yards with this .22," I chuckled aloud.

After the disaster when the cats ate my frozen squirrels, I had learned to skin my own squirrels. In fact, I could actually skin them while I walked and hunted. Before long, I draped the skinned carcass over a sapling, as a fresh warm meal for the whisky-jack that fluttered from branch to branch, accompanying me through the bush. Then I tucked the pelt from my first squirrel into my knapsack. As I continued on my way, I finished plucking the partridge and stuffed it into the knapsack with the squirrel pelt.

Following my trapline and the chattering squirrels, I pushed forward, through the melting snow, across the south end of Taylor's farm to Bench Creek. I turned upstream along the creek to the school section. Nobody lived on it, as it was land that had been set aside for future schools. I crossed the road to the Princes' farm, hunting from one stand of spruce to the next. By the time I reached the South Road again, I had four squirrels and one partridge. I crossed the South Road and continued along Bench Creek to Sliva's land. There, I continued to hunt as I picked up the old trail that would take me back to the Stump Farm.

Mom wasn't home when I arrived, but I knew that she was going to be surprised when she learned of my successful day. All told, I had shot five squirrels and picked another out of a trap. I had one partridge and a fool hen. Fool hens weren't as good eating as partridge because they ate spruce needles and had a pretty strong taste. But Mom would fix that, coating each piece in flour and spices, and roasting them with a mess of onions until they were the tenderest of morsels. Oh man, I could already taste the feed we were going to have for supper.

After I arrived back at the log house, I was getting my surprise ready for Mom. I had stretched the squirrels I had shot, and the one from the trap was thawing out on the floor beside the stove. The birds were plucked and drawn. I allowed myself the pleasure of pausing to admire the birds, the gizzards, the hearts, and the livers.

"It's a good thing you're a good shot, Bobby my boy," I crowed, patting myself on the back. "Look at that, not a bit of meat wasted."

I had been so engrossed in congratulating myself that I never even heard the car pull into the driveway, but I heard the door slam. I looked out the window and saw Mom getting out of a car. She was home earlier than expected.

Mom bailed out of that car and raced towards the house. I watched as she zipped past the window, heading for the door. I turned to face her. I was so excited, I couldn't wait to tell her about my day. For some dumb reason, I had completely forgotten that I was sick, and I was standing there in the middle of the kitchen with a bird in each hand, grinning like a Cheshire cat, when Mom bolted through the door.

Mom took one step inside, then stopped as if she had been hit with a shovel. Man, she couldn't believe her eyes when she saw what I had got for supper. Her mouth dropped open and just hung there. Mom was speechless.

Her friend Agnes, who had walked in right behind her, took one look at me and howled with laughter. Agnes couldn't believe what she was seeing either. She grabbed a chair and sat down to keep from keeling over with laughter.

"Bobby, what are you doing? I . . . I thought you were sick in bed," Mom stammered when she was finally able to speak.

"I'm feeling much better now," I replied happily. "And look, Mom, look what I got us for supper!" I held out the two birds.

"Here I am, worried sick about you, and . . . and you're out playing around," Mom said, ignoring our supper. The surprise and shock had disappeared from her voice. It was replaced by anger. Indisputable anger. I don't know that I had ever seen Mom so angry.

"See, Florence, I told you . . . I told you not to worry, that he'd be okay," said Agnes, adding her two cents' worth between bursts of laughter. "I've got kids of my own, and they're never as sick as they make out."

"I . . . I got a half a dozen squirrels too, Mom," I quickly chimed in.

"You . . . you're supposed to be sick," Mom snapped. "You stayed home today because you were sick."

"Yeah, I know. But I'm better now. I feel great." I smiled. "Look, I've cleaned the chickens, and I've only got one more squirrel to skin."

"You're sick. You're sick, and when you're sick, you go to bed and . . . and you stay in bed," Mom snapped at me. "Now, you get back into that bed this instant." It was pretty obvious that Mom was not nearly as happy as I was about the two birds and the six squirrels.

"I'm okay, Mom. Honest I am," I assured her. "I was just gonna skin the last squirrel."

"You get back into that bed, or I'll . . . I'll skin *you*," Mom said angrily.

For some reason, Mom was not as convinced as I was that my health had improved. Before I knew what was happening, I was back in the bed. Mom never said a word as she rubbed my chest and crammed a hot towel up under my pyjamas, then smeared a big gob of Vicks up my nose. Instantly, I was sweating like a hog.

Later, when the kids returned from school, the smell of roasting partridge drifted into the bedroom. I was wringing wet with sweat, but I was ready to get up and tackle a heaping helping of that supper.

When I heard my brother and sisters at the table, I knew supper was served. I figured it was just an oversight that I hadn't been called, but I certainly knew enough to get to the table at mealtime. I was just putting on my pants when Mom walked into the room with a tray.

"And just what do you think you're doing, young man?" Mom asked.

"I was getting up to have supper," I replied.

"Not when you're sick, you're not," Mom stated quite sternly. "When you're sick you get supper in bed. Now get back in that bed."

Well, I had to admit, roast chicken would taste just as good in bed as it would at the table. After all, I smiled smugly, I was the sick one and I was getting my supper in bed. Mom set down the tray on a chair beside the bed and walked out of the room.

"Mom," I called to her when I looked at my plate.

"What do you want now?" she asked as she came back into the room.

"I've only got soup," I replied. "I didn't get no partridge."

"That's right," she answered. "You're sick, remember, and when you're sick, you get a nice bowl of hot soup. I'm sure you'll feel much better after you eat." Before she left the room, she replaced the towel and jammed another gob of Vicks up my nose.

I sat and looked at that miserable bowl of soup. I knew that in the morning I would be going to school. The only way that I wouldn't be going to school was if I woke up dead.

SHAKE A LEG

"C'mon, Bob, shake a leg." It was Dad's voice that woke me from a deep sleep. I opened my eyes. The dull glow from the coal-oil lamp barely cast any light into the tiny bedroom. "C'mon," he called again. "It's time to rise and shine."

I moaned as I reached back and grabbed for my cap. I had got into the habit of wearing my cap to bed – that way, it was easy to find in the morning, and if I was lucky, I could get out of the house before Mom made me comb my hair. With my cap planted firmly on my head, I pulled on my socks, my shirt, and a pair of bibbed coveralls. Coveralls were the order of dress whenever we worked in the fields. Everybody wore coveralls. I wore coveralls. I hated coveralls.

My coveralls were several sizes too big. That was not an accident. I was growing like a weed, or so I had been told, and I would grow into them. The oversized baggy coveralls hung on my body like an extra-large gunny sack. I rolled up the pant legs, several rolls, until each pant leg hung to about my ankles. I stood up and the bib fell forward. It hung open like a scoop shovel, ready to catch everything. I could look right down the front. I could see down to my shirt-tail. I could see down to my . . . well, I could see down both pant legs all the way to my boots. I could even see the linoleum on the floor. The only good thing about coveralls was that dirt, hay, and straw, everything could fall into the bib and drop right through the bulky legs all the way to the ground, without ever touching a person's body. Dad had often told me to wear long johns when I wore my coveralls. But long johns were worse than coveralls—they were the itchiest things I had ever worn. Long johns were woolly, and so scratchy they just about drove me crazy when I wore them. It was bad enough having to wear them during the winter when the temperature plunged, but unless someone held me down and forced them on me, there was no way I would wear long johns in warm weather.

It was fall on the Stump Farm, and fall was harvest time. Everyone was busy bringing in the crops. Everyone, that is, but us on the Stump Farm. Some of our land had been cleared. In fact, my poor old father very nearly broke his back clearing the brush and trees, pulling the stumps, and breaking that land. However, we were rapidly discovering that very little grew in that muskeg. It was a different picture on the neighbours' land, especially the land across the South Road. Their land was higher, and they had crops. However, our own lack of a crop never prevented us from helping with the harvest.

I could not remember a time when Dad was not at home for the harvest. He would not leave for the bush camp until freeze-up, usually long after the harvest. Dad always felt that it was not only neighbourly, it was our duty to help bring in the crop. After all, that's what good neighbours were for. They always helped each other.

"Can I go too, Dad?" I asked when I heard he was going harvesting.

"I think so," he replied, nodding his head. "I think you're old enough to work with the men in the field now."

"Oh, boy!" I shouted happily. "Does that mean I get my own pitchfork?"

"Not so fast," Mom quickly added her two cents' worth. "I think you're just a little young to be tossing a pitchfork around."

"I can handle a pitchfork," I argued. "Can't I, Dad?"

"I think you'll do just fine," he replied.

"Well, I don't think so," Mom stated emphatically. Mom always had some pretty strong ideas of what her kids could and couldn't do – and right now, it appeared that my using a pitchfork on the threshing crew was not one of the could's.

"I can too," I argued. "I use one all the time when I feed the cows."

"Feeding the cows is a lot different than pitching bundles," Mom replied.

"Please, Dad," I pleaded.

"It's okay, Florence. He'll be all right with me," Dad said calmly. "I think it's time he faced up to a man's job."

"Yeah!" I yelled happily. "I'm going harvesting with Dad." Dad and I had won.

Suddenly, I could see myself in the field. With one simple little thrust of my trusty pitchfork, I plucked a bundle of wheat from a stook like it was a feather. In the same smooth motion, I flipped the bundle high into the air and watched it land in the centre of the hayrack. Oh yeah, I was ready to pitch bundles.

"We'll see how happy you are tomorrow night when you drag yourself through that door," Mom said . She sat there looking at me, giving me that you're-just-my-little-boy-yet look. "Pitching bundles is a lot tougher than what you've been used to doing. I don't think you're ready for it."

"I can handle it," I warbled. "You'll see, Mom. You come out to the field and watch me toss those old bundles on the hayrack."

So on this Saturday morning, we good neighbours would soon be off to the field across the road, to help with the threshing of a neighbour's wheat crop.

As I stumbled out of the bedroom into the kitchen, I knew that today was a big day in my life. Larry followed, charging out close on my heels, and plunked himself down on a chair beside me.

"Are you gonna stay and work all day, Rob?" he asked excitedly.

"You betcha," I chortled. "I'm gonna work with the

men. I even get to have my own pitchfork an' . . . an' everything. I'll betcha I can pitch bundles as good as the men."

"Wow," he replied. "I wish I could come too. I betcha I could pitch bundles with the men too."

"In a couple of years you can," I replied knowledgeably. "In a couple of years, when you're older like me. But first things first, Larry. A man can't work on an empty stomach, ya know." The first order of business was to eat a good breakfast.

"Here you go," Dad chuckled. "This oughta stick to your ribs." It was one of Dad's favourite expressions, for he knew, as did everyone else, that his pancakes were the rib-stickin' kind. He flipped a huge pancake onto the plate in front of me. The pancake was a monster, about the same size as the frying pan. It just about covered the whole plate. Dad didn't believe in making a bunch of little pancakes when one big one would do the job.

"There you go now, eat up," he said. A pot of homemade syrup (brown sugar mixed with boiling water) was on the table. I poured syrup on that pancake. Syrup flowed over the pancake and over the plate. Syrup flowed over the sides of the plate and onto the table. I poured syrup on that pancake until it just about floated. When I felt certain that there was enough syrup on the pancake, on the plate, and on the table, I wolfed it down. The plate-sized pancake quickly disappeared, and there were still a few ribs that had nothing sticking to them. I asked for seconds and reached for more syrup. When the second pancake and the syrup were gone, my ribs were really stuck together. It was time to go threshing . . . .

It was not the first time I had ventured over to the neighbour's wheat field. I had already made several trips, sometimes alone, sometimes with Larry, and once with Dad.

Earlier in the fall, Dad and I had gone over to help cut the crop. I knew that the neighbour had to be the richest, luckiest man in the world. He was the man who owned the land, he owned the wheat crop, and he also owned a binder. Being the owner of everything, he got to ride on the binder. All day long, he rode around and around his field. His team of horses plodded along, pulling his binder behind them. The mower part cut into the standing wheat, the long arms of the reel laid the cut grain onto the table, and the canvas belt carried the wheat into the binder. There, it was wrapped with binder twine into neat bundles—sheaves, as some folks called them—then the binder tossed the bundles out onto the ground. That was where we came in. We good neighbours got to walk around behind his horses, behind his binder, behind the neighbour sitting on the binder, and we picked up his bundles. We would gather ten or twelve of them and stand them on end, leaning them in to form little teepees—stooks, they were called. The heads of the grain in the stooks had to be pointing up, up towards the sky, up to the sun, up so that the wheat would dry before being threshed.

On one memorable occasion, my brother Larry and I had taken particular notice of the stooks in the neighbour's field. We had intended to go fishing in Bench Creek, but for some reason we got sidetracked. World War II had ended, but not in the minds of young boys, and it was the War that made us do it. As we strolled across the field, through the stooks, we got to talking about the War. The game started out innocently enough.

"Hey, Rob, do you see that?" Larry suddenly yelled out. He pointed ahead to a stook.

"What?" I asked. I looked where he was pointing, but saw nothing, only a stook of wheat.

"There," he cautioned me. "Behind that stook. It looks like there's a Kraut waiting to get us." Larry fell behind a stook, out of sight of the imaginary Kraut.

"Yeah," I responded. Then I dove behind the closest stook. I didn't want to give the Kraut anything to shoot at.

We carefully peered out around the side of the stooks.

"He's not looking," Larry whispered. We both crouched low and moved forward, darting from stook to stook, towards the Kraut. When we finally arrived at his hiding spot, we found he had moved. It was a game of cat and mouse with the wily Kraut. We knew he was there somewhere, and soon we were racing forward, darting out from one stook and diving in behind the next, searching for that sneaky Kraut. We were doing a masterful job without being detected.

Yes, it was innocent enough, all right, until one particular dive, a long, badly judged dive. Larry and I both picked the same stook to hide behind. We collided in mid-air as we dove forward. We crashed into the stook. Instantly, there were little Kraut-hunters and bundles sprawled out in the stubble. We had carelessly and foolishly exposed ourselves to the enemy, who was quickly forgotten while we hurriedly restored the stook to its former position.

But now that he had seen us, the enemy was shooting. We were running and diving, and soon every dive took us into a stook. Before long, we had run and dived our way through the whole Kraut army finally reaching the safety of the pine trees at the far end of the field. There, in the safety of the forest, away from the prying eyes and the bullets of the Kraut, we could rest. Larry and I were sitting, relaxing, leaning our backs against a pine tree, enjoying our victory over the Krauts.

"What do you boys think you're doing?" a booming voice suddenly roared, shaking the pines.

That unexpected bellow just about scared the life right out of me. I bolted to my feet and turned to face the voice. It was worse than the Krauts—it was the neighbour. I wanted to run, but my knees were shaking so badly they were knocking, and my legs wouldn't work.

"I . . . I . . ." I opened my mouth to say something, although I wasn't sure what. Maybe he'd understand if I told him there had been a war out there, and that we had just eluded the enemy. But other than a couple of weak I's, nothing came out.

"Who knocked over my stooks?" he roared as he surveyed his field.

I, too, turned to look out across the field. It was easy to see where the war had taken us. In the field, neatly covered with stooks, was a line of scattered bundles. The line of destruction came straight across the field and pointed into the pine trees, right to the spot where we had stopped to rest.

"I . . . I . . ." Again I tried to tell him, but still nothing came out.

"Well?" his voice roared. I was so scared, I just about fell over.

"I . . . it . . . it was some k-kids from t-town," I finally squeaked out. We saw 'em an' we . . . we was chasin' 'em, b-but they got away."

"You boys better get your butts off of my land, before I tan your backsides!" he barked angrily.

I didn't try to say anything this time. My legs, which had been feeling pretty weak, suddenly found new strength. I spun on my heels and raced for home. Larry hadn't tried to say anything—he had just turned and run. He was already several steps ahead of me, and try as I might, I couldn't catch him. Man, can that little bugger ever run, I moaned to myself as I raced after him. This time, as we beat our retreat across the field, we knew where the enemy was and we knew who he was. He was behind us, he was our neighbour, and there was no need to dive into the stooks for protection. Except for giving the stooks a wide berth as we ran by them, we headed straight for the Stump Farm . . . .

Suddenly, I was a little tentative about my first day pitching bundles. I was even more tentative about confronting the neighbour. I hadn't told Dad what we had done, and I didn't know if the neighbour had either. But I knew that Dad would certainly have something to say about the line of destruction that had marked our war game.

The threshing machine was set up and ready to go when we walked into the field. I took a quick glance down the field and was relieved to see that all the stooks had been rebuilt. Then I noticed the horses beside the threshing machine. There were three teams of horses hitched to hayracks. I immediately, forgot about the knocked-down stooks when I noticed that one of the teams belonged to Grandfather. My day was made. I knew right away where I was going to be and who I would be tossing bundles for. With my pitchfork in hand, I raced across the field towards Grandfather and his team being careful not to get too close to the stooks.

However, before I got to Grandfather's team, I stopped. Right beside the threshing machine, I spotted apples. Huge, red, ripe, Delicious apples. There was a whole box of them. I had never seen a whole box of apples, except in the store. And here, right before my eyes, was a box with apples heaped to the top. I loved apples, especially Delicious apples. Just standing there looking, I could already taste them. I was torn between that box of apples and Grandfather's team.

"Do you want an apple, Boy?" Grandfather laughed when he saw me eyeing that box.

"Uh-huh," I mumbled. "I sure do."

"Well, let's see," he replied. "Are you workin' t'day,

Boy, or are you here to play?"

"I'm a working man, Grandfather," I replied. "I'm here to work."

"What're you gonna do with them stooks today, Boy?" he asked. He put his hands on his knees and leaned over so he could look me square in the eye. And he laughed.

"I'm gonna pitch them onto the hayracks," I replied. Suddenly, I was wondering if Grandfather knew about the Krauts and the stooks.

"That's m'boy!" he roared approvingly. "That's what I want to hear. You just git on over there and help yerself, Boy," he laughed. "Those apples are for the workin' men."

I started towards that box of apples, then stopped. The apples had a guard, the neighbour. Suddenly, I wasn't hungry for an apple.

"C'mon, boy. Get yourself an apple," growled the neighbour when he saw me hesitate.

I approached him and that apple box with a lot of caution. Once again my knees were weak as I slowly bent over, picked up an apple, and backed up to Grandfather and safety. I never took my eyes off the neighbour the whole time.

Back at Grandfather's side, I was enjoying the best of both worlds. I was busy making short work of that apple and anxious to start pitching bundles onto Grandfather's hayrack.

However, all good things must come to an end, and I was crushed when I learned that it was not I who chose who I worked with—the neighbour made those decisions. After all, it was his land and his wheat. With heavy heart, I watched as Grandfather and his crew pulled away from the threshing machine. I tramped along beside Dad, and we followed a different team out to pick up bundles. I knew that Grandfather's team would get far more bundles than we would. It was a sad start to a long day.

Our driver stopped the team at the first stook, then he grabbed a pitchfork and jumped to the ground. I watched as Dad picked a bundle out of the stook. His pitchfork barely seemed to tickle the bundle as he easily flipped it onto the hayrack. Then the driver plucked out a bundle which he, too, easily flipped onto the hayrack.

I stabbed my pitchfork into a bundle, driving it in deep, right up to the hilt, and in one fluid motion spun to flip it onto the hayrack. But the stupid bundle that I had chosen was far heavier than the ones that Dad and the driver had picked up. In one fluid motion I had spun, lost my grip on the pitchfork, and flung myself face-first on the ground. My pitchfork remained, lodged firmly in the stook. I jumped to my feet, grabbed my stupid pitchfork, and put all my strength into plucking a bundle off that stook. I grunted and groaned and strained every muscle in my body. I could feel the pancakes pulling away from my ribs as I struggled to lift that miserable bundle, but there was no way it was moving.

"Just a minute, Bob," Dad laughed. "You're trying to lift the whole stook. Pull that fork back a bit, and just take one bundle at a time."

"Okay," I muttered. I pulled the pitchfork back, until

most of the tines were showing. Then I gave another mighty heave. The single bundle suddenly burst free. I wasn't expecting it, and it shot up so fast that I lost my balance.

"Watch out, kid!" the driver yelled. He recoiled as if he had been snake-bitten, as my pitchfork and the bundle whizzed up past his ear. "You better watch where you're sticking that fork."

Up, higher, into the air went my pitchfork. Up, higher, into the air went the bundle. I started to lose my balance, to fall over backwards. My little legs started to backpedal as I fought gamely to keep my feet under me. I was rapidly moving in the wrong direction, away from the hayrack. After some furious leg-pumping, I was just about managing to get the pitchfork and the bundle under control, when that bundle on the end of my pitchfork took over. The stupid thing had a mind of its own, and it started to fall forward. Ahead of me, I could see the hayrack. I knew that if I was fast enough, I could get that bundle onto the hayrack where it belonged. I started to run forward, as fast as I could, but that stupid bundle kept falling. Suddenly, I could see Dad in front of me. His eyes were wide open in shock when he realized that the bundle, the pitchfork, and I were bearing down on him.

"Drop it, Bob!" Dad yelled when I almost stuck him on the end of my pitchfork, right next to the bundle of wheat.

Lucky for Dad, the bundle hit the ground in front of him. Unlucky for me, I was still running forward when the pitchfork stuck into the ground. The end of the handle buried itself in my stomach. It felt as if the handle was lodged about the same place where the pancakes were sticking to my ribs.

"Ooof," I moaned as the air shot out of my lungs. My knees buckled, and I collapsed on the ground.

"Are you okay, Bob?" Dad asked. He was concerned, but I could see a faint smile tickle the corners of his lips.

"I'm okay," I groaned. "I think I'm dying, but I'll be okay."

"Well, then you better get up and get moving. There's a lot of work to do."

"Yeah, and you better watch where you point that pitchfork," warned the driver. "I don't want to get laid up because of no fool kid."

"I'm okay," I groaned again as I tried to force some air back into my lungs. I stood up and tried to walk as if nothing had happened. But I could only stumble around the stook while Dad and the driver loaded the last of the bundles. Then I stumbled after the wagon.

"Have you ever seen so many mice in your life?" the driver asked.

"There's a lot of them, all right," Dad replied.

"Where?" I asked. "I don't see no mice."

"That's because you were stumbling around like a drunken sailor," mocked the driver. He had suddenly lightened up and he faked stumbling forward to the next stook. "When I picked up that last bundle, there must have been a hundred of them running around."

At the next stook, I made sure that I was watching when the last bundle was picked up. Sure enough, there were mice scurrying everywhere. Mice ran under the wagon. They ran under the horses. They ran through the stubble, heading for the next stook. I ran after them, stabbing at them with the pitchfork. I would have done better stabbing the bundles—at least they didn't move.

Before long, I heard the tractor start up, and then the rattle and clanging of machinery. The old threshing machine was running and ready for action. A glance confirmed what I already knew—Grandfather and his crew were the first ones back, their wagon loaded with bundles. As we neared the threshing machine with our load, we could hear a lot of yelling and cursing.

"Hurry up, you old bugger!" I heard the man running the threshing machine yell. "I got more fields to thresh before the snow flies. Hurry up, you're holdin' up the works."

"Who you callin' an old bugger?" Grandfather roared back. Grandfather always talked and joked a lot, but he always did his fair share, and he never did take kindly to criticism.

"You," snarled the operator. "Hurry up now, toss them bundles in there, smart-like. Look at all the wagons coming in. You're slowin' us down. At the rate you're goin', I'll be here 'til Christmas."

"I'll show you who's an old bugger," Grandfather snorted. He dug into his load like a man possessed. Suddenly, the threshing machine started to buck and snort. There was a terrible sound, a groaning, from deep inside the threshing machine.

"What the—" yelled the operator, as he rushed to shut it down.

"Har, har, har!" Grandfather roared.

"You threw a bundle in backwards," yelled the operator.

"I did not. I wasn't born yesterday, Boy," Grandfather chuckled triumphantly. "I learned a long time ago how to deal with the likes of you. Remember, Boy, I was threshin' when you was still wearin' three-cornered pants." Then Grandfather turned towards our wagon.

"C'mon, Boy," he called to me and laughed. "Let's git us an apple. It looks like we'll have us a bit of a wait, while the hotshot unplugs that machine."

"Did you throw a bundle in backwards, Grandfather?" I asked.

"You know, Boy," Grandfather laughed. "when you're as old as I am, you learn that if you're gonna do somethin', you do it right. Now, if you want to plug up a threshing machine, you don't throw a bundle in backwards."

"You don't?" I asked. I took another look at the operator. He was cussing and swearing, making rude comments about Grandfather's background.

"No, Boy," Grandfather said smugly. "You throw three of 'em in, an' all three of 'em go in backwards. That plugs it up real good."

"Wow," I replied. It only served to confirm what I already knew. Grandfather was the smartest guy in the whole world.

It was getting close to noon. We had flipped the last bundle out of the hayrack and were getting ready to head out for another load. Although I had already eaten six or seven apples, I was hungry; and to make matters worse, I was tired. In fact, Mom was right, I was getting sick and tired of pitching bundles. I was just about to head to the box for another apple when the neighbour called out.

"Just a minute there!"

"Whoa!" the driver yelled at the horses.

"You fellas, you better get yourself some lunch—" he began.

"Whoopee!" I yodelled. I, for one, was very happy for the break.

"After lunch, I want you boys to check out a row of stooks I marked on the far side of the field," said the neighbour. "You'll be able to see the ones I mean—I put a stake at both ends."

"Why's that?" asked the driver. "You don't want them picked up?"

"Oh yeah, I want them picked up, all right. I just don't know if they're ready. That row got knocked over by some kids a while back," he replied. He paused and looked right at me. I moved in behind Dad.

Suddenly, I wished I had listened to Mom. I wished I was anywhere but in that bloody field being a good neighbour. My stomach was churning. I didn't feel like eating. I wasn't hungry. I was feeling sick as I thought about that row of stooks.

"I just want you to check them. If they're ready, pick 'em up and bring 'em in."

"What do we do if the bundles are still green?" asked the driver.

"Leave 'em," answered the neighbour. He never

even hesitated in his answer. "If they're still green, I'll just have to bring back the crew to pick 'em up later."

"On no," I moaned. "That means I'll have to come back too."

"C'mon, Bob. Shake a leg," Dad called. "Let's get us some grub and get back out there."

I shuffled over to a big pot of stew. I couldn't eat stew. I looked at the stack of sandwiches. I couldn't eat a sandwich. I looked at a huge chocolate cake with thick chocolate icing. But I couldn't eat any cake either. By the time we were ready to hit the field again, I hadn't eaten anything.

"What's the matter, boy? You eat too many apples?" teased the driver.

"Yeah," I mumbled. "I think so."

It was a long trip over to the marked row of stooks. Reluctantly, I trudged along behind the team and wagon, and I cursed every Kraut that had ever lived. I was dreading the very thought of looking at that first stook. There was no doubt in my mind that every bundle was still going to be green. I don't mind saying that a load was lifted off my shoulders when Dad and the driver started to flip bundle after bundle from the first stook into the hayrack.

After picking up the marked row, our crew continued to operate in the far end of the field. Dad and I no longer walked along behind the wagon. Actually, I was so tired I couldn't walk. I could barely crawl onto the wagon for the free ride. And not having eaten any lunch, I was famished.

I was on my umpteenth apple when we arrived to

pick up another load. Dad and the driver were pitching bundles while I stood back and polished off the apple. I guess I was more concerned with the apple than what was going on, and I hardly noticed that they were moving ahead.

Suddenly, I had the strangest feeling on my leg. Inside the baggy legs of those bibbed coveralls, I felt a scurrying mass of fur. I felt it brush against my skin in several places. I felt fur tickle my ankle, my shin, my knee. I had company, unwanted company, inside my pant leg.

"Eeyiiikes!" I yelled. My pitchfork flew from my hands, and I jumped about four feet straight up in the air. While I was in the air, I pounded that pant leg with both hands. I landed on the ground with a thud, and instantly I realized that I should have listened to Dad. I should have worn my long johns, for suddenly that scurrying mass of fur sprouted little sharp things. Claws. Claws were digging into my leg. I pumped my leg up and down like a crazy man. I stamped my foot and jumped around like a person possessed, trying to shake that little devil. But the more I jumped and stomped, the harder he dug in.

Stomping and shaking that leg only resulted in the rolled-up leg of the coveralls coming down. The long leg flopped over my foot and flapped about until I accidentally stepped on it. The next thing I knew, I was flat on my face on the ground. I lay there for a second, waiting. There was nothing. No little claws in my legs. All seemed quiet on the leg front.

I realized that somewhere, someone was laughing.

I drew in a deep breath, relieved that my ordeal with the mouse was over. But then I felt it again, the unmistakable feel of fur brushing against my bare knee. The little mouse was still scooting around inside my coveralls. I leapt to my feet and once more beat furiously on my pant leg. I pounded as fast and as hard as I could, but that mouse was a slippery little devil. He must have seen every blow coming, for each blow landed where the mouse had been. He scurried around on my leg, inside my coveralls, as if he knew exactly what he was doing. I was having a devil of a time trying to shake that little mouse.

Finally, a lucky blow caught up with him. I felt a hot, furry little body squish against my leg. The clawing stopped. I shook my leg vigorously and watched as the squashed mouse slid out the bottom of my pant leg. I pulled out the bib on my coveralls and looked down. I breathed a sigh of relief. I was still all there.

In the distance, the laughter had grown to a roar. Even Dad was smiling. But the driver was bent over double. He was killing himself.

"Hotdang!" he howled. "I didn't think the kid had that much energy left in him. Man, that's about the funniest damn thing I ever saw," he hooted as he slowly rolled over into the stubble.

"That's pretty funny, all right," Dad chuckled. Even he had to stop for a few minutes and laugh.

"Did you ever see anything like that in your life?" hooted the driver. He was lying on the ground holding his sides.

"I don't see what's so funny," I snorted. "That

stupid mouse could have bit me . . . bit my . . . Well, it's not funny, you know!"

"C'mon, Bob," Dad called. He was struggling to keep a straight face. "It's time to shake a leg."

"I'm comin'," I moaned, and slowly I trudged after the wagon.

It was after dark when the last bundle had been pitched into the threshing machine. The men sat around. They drank hot coffee and they laughed and joked. To them it was just another day's work. I flopped on the ground. This was more than just another day to me. I was dead tired. My hands were so sore from holding that pitchfork all day, I could barely straighten them out.

"I'm pooped, Dad," I mumbled into the darkness. "Let's go home."

Finally, we arrived back at the house. Everyone was asleep. It was almost as if the house was abandoned. The coal-oil lantern burning on the table had been turned down, the faint glow throwing barely any light. Most of the house was in complete darkness, and it was quiet. I had never experienced the house like this, and it gave me an eerie, creepy feeling.

"Mmmm, just take a whiff of that," Dad chuckled as he lifted the lid from a pot on the back of the stove.

"Of what?" I asked.

"Deer stew," he replied and smacked his lips. "Now that smells good!"

"I'm starved," I moaned as I dropped my exhausted body on a chair by the table.

"Here's a plate. C'mon and dig in," Dad yodelled as

he set a plate on the table in front of me. He hummed an old cowboy song as he scooped deer stew onto his plate.

"Okay," I mumbled. Man, am I tired, I thought. I reached for the plate with my poor, sore, swollen hands. Just that little movement reminded me of the torture I had endured. A sharp pain shot up right between my shoulder blades. My legs were all scratched from the wayward mouse. I was a mess. I slowly lowered my head and laid it on the table.

Suddenly, I awoke with a start. Something was wrong. I sat bolt upright in bed. Every muscle in my body rebelled.

"Oh, man," I groaned.

"Hey, Rob," Larry greeted me, "how did the harvest go?" Larry was still excited.

"Leave me alone," I moaned. I looked around and wondered how I had ended up in bed.

"C'mon, get up," he warbled. "It's almost noon. C'mon, Rob, people die in bed, you know."

"I know," my voice cracked. I tried to move in the bed. My body didn't obey. Every muscle was throbbing. I tried to open my hands, but they wouldn't budge. I looked at them.

"C'mon, Rob, tell me what it's like to work with the men. Was harvesting as great as you thought it'd be?"

"Look at my hands!" I almost cried as I shoved them out for Larry to look at.

"Holy!" he exclaimed. "They look like one big blister."

"I know. And I can tell you one thing for sure."

"What's that?" he asked.

"Harvesting is not what it's cracked up to be. If the Krauts and the neighbour don't get you, the mice and the pitchforks will. From now on, somebody else can do the harvesting. I'm gonna stay home and do my chores." Suddenly, I felt again the pain that had awakened me. I leapt out of bed.

"Where you goin', Rob?" Larry yelled. He was certainly impressed with my renewed vigor. I charged past him and bolted out the door.

This was no time to dally. I didn't have time to explain the consequences of munching Delicious apples for a whole day.

TEMPTING MORSELS

"Hey, Grandfather," I called a greeting as I raced into his yard, "I need your .22 and I come to borrow it."

"Again?" Grandfather laughed. "You want to borrow my .22 again?"

"Yeah, and I need it right away," I replied.

"I don't know, Boy," he answered, shaking his head. "I just might have to think on that for a bit."

"Please, Grandfather," I pleaded.

"You know, Boy, if memory serves me right, I had to go and get that gun back the last time you borrowed it," he said, still shaking his head and thinking.

"I know," I mumbled. "Mom said I could keep it for a while. She said she didn't think you'd be needing that old gun anyway."

"I know, Boy, I know what your mother said. But your mother doesn't own the gun. It's my gun and you have to learn to return it when you finish usin' it."

"But I only kept it so's I could shoot some partridge to eat," I said.

"Uh-huh, and what do you want to shoot this time?" he asked. "More partridge?"

"Nope, squirrels," I replied quickly. "The squirrels are prime, and I'm gonna shoot me some before they den up for the winter. If I can get enough squirrel skins, I'll be able to buy my own .22, and then I won't have to borrow yours no more."

"Well, I guess I can let you use it one more time," Grandfather replied. "But I want you to promise me one thing, Boy."

"You bet, Grandfather," I replied, happy to be getting my hands on the .22 once again. "You just name it."

"You tell your mother that I'll be comin' up for supper."

"I'll tell her, Grandfather," I sang out happily. "You can count on me. I'll tell her that you'll be up tonight for supper." Boy, this was great, I thought. Not only was I getting the .22 again, but Grandfather was coming to our place for supper.

"No. No, Boy, you tell her that I'll be there tomorrow night, and I'll be looking for some fresh squirrel stew," he said, smacking his lips.

"Squirrel stew?" I repeated. "Did you say 'squirrel stew', Grandfather?"

"You heard me right, Boy. Your mother makes the best squirrel stew, you know. Now you go and get that .22, and don't forget to tell your mother what I said."

He laughed. "Mmm-mmm," he smacked his lips again, then turned and walked away.

"Oh yeah, sure I will," I mumbled. But I had a long memory, and I was thinking back to the last squirrel stew episode. Back to a time when I was a lot younger and a little more gullible . . . .

"Bobby," Mom stated very firmly. "This is the last time I'm telling you – you get back into your room and into bed before I tan your backside. I've already told you there'll be no more to eat tonight."

Mom sounded suspiciously as if she had reached the end of her rope. Her voice had a weary, no-nonsense tone. The look on her face was the look of total frustration. And why not? For the past couple of hours, ever since she had tucked me into bed, and kissed me goodnight, she had told me repeatedly to stay in bed. But my mainspring was coiled so tight, I was wound up like a clock. I had stretched her patience to the limit, and this warning sounded as if it was final. There would be no more. There would be consequences, severe consequences, if I were to stray from my bed once more.

It really wasn't my fault that I was unable to stay in bed. It was Dad's fault. Dad was the reason that I kept getting up and parting the sheets that hung from a rope stretched the length of the cabin. The sheets served as wall and door, dividing the cabin. It was through these sheets that I wandered out into the dim light of the coal-oil lantern.

It had all started earlier that evening, when our door

suddenly flew open and a flour sack sailed in out of the night, landed on the floor with a thud, and skidded right over to the kitchen stove. The flour sack was followed by a familiar figure.

"Dad!" we all shouted at once. Chairs crashed to the floor, as we all made a beeline for the door. Dad was home for an unscheduled visit, one of his infrequent visits from the lumber camp. I couldn't believe it when I found out he was home for the whole night. I was really excited to see Dad, but I was even more curious to see what was in that flour sack lying in the middle of the floor.

"What's in the sack, Dad?" I asked.

"I'm hungry," he replied, ignoring my question. "What's for supper?"

"I don't know," Mom teased. "We didn't know you were coming. I'm not sure there's enough for you."

"Ye gods and little fishes!" Dad exclaimed. "Don't tell me I drove all this way for nothing."

"I don't know," Mom laughed happily. "What do you kids think? Do you think there's enough for Dad?"

"Here, Dad, you can have mine." I offered him my plate, knowing he wouldn't take it. "What's in the sack?" I asked again. I was so curious to know what was in the sack, I couldn't have eaten another bite. I was working my way over to the stove for a better look.

"In that old sack?" he chuckled and pointed to the flour sack that lay beside the cookstove. "Oh, I wasn't sure if there was going to be any supper left by the time I got here, so I thought maybe I had just better bring my own."

"Bobby, you sit down and eat your supper. There's lots here for your father," Mom replied. One thing was certain: We didn't have much money, but at our table there was always enough for one or two more. And for sure, there was always enough for Dad, whether Mom knew he was coming or not.

I looked at Dad, then I looked back at that old flour sack lying on the floor. Was Dad kidding me? Was that really his supper lying there on the floor? It was a big sack all right—about a fifty-pounder, and it looked as if it was pretty full.

"Hoo hoo," I yodelled. "If that's Dad's supper, I'll bet there's enough for everyone."

It wasn't uncommon to carry lunch in a flour sack. I saw lots of the men who loaded railroad ties down at the landing carry their lunch in flour sacks. When I went to school, some of the kids even used flour sacks to carry their lunch in. But rarely had I seen anybody throw his lunch sack through the door and onto the floor.

"Is that really your supper, Dad?" I asked. I couldn't take my eyes off the sack.

"Oh, you betcha, those are tempting morsels," Dad chuckled. "I got all the makin's of a good, lip-smackin' meal in that sack."

"Wow!" I replied. Once more I started for the sack.

"Bob," Mom scolded my dad, "don't go telling him that. You know he believes every word you say."

"Don't go telling me what, Mom?" I asked.

"Never mind," she replied. "C'mon back to the table and finish your supper. C'mon, everybody, back to the table. Your supper is getting cold." While Mom spoke, she was busy rearranging the table, setting a place for Dad.

But I was no longer hungry, and I couldn't get the sack out of my mind. "Tempting morsels", whatever that was. That sack was awfully intriguing for a six-year-old.

Finally, supper was over. Now it was time to examine the flour sack and its contents. Dad walked over to the cookstove and picked up the sack. He lifted it up and untied the piece of cord that held it shut. Then he shook the contents out onto the floor.

Little balls of fur dropped from the sack. Each one clunked and bounced on the linoleum. The flour sack was full of squirrels. Little red squirrels. And each one frozen, solid as a rock, into a little round furry ball.

"But . . . but Dad, those are all squirrels," I stammered. I couldn't hide my disappointment. "They don't look like no tempting morsels to me."

"They don't?" he said and looked surprised. "You mean your mother hasn't cooked you up a mess of squirrels?" Dad looked very serious.

"No," I replied. "We don't eat squirrels . . . do we?" I looked long and hard at Mom. I couldn't help but wonder, had she been holding out on me? Mom rolled her eyes and looked to the heavens.

"Well, gee willikers!" Dad replied. "I was sure I asked your mother to cook you up a mess of squirrels." He shook his head. I could see the disappointment in his eyes. I knew that Dad always trapped squirrels in the winter to sell their hides. I even remembered how happy he'd been once when one pelt had brought a whopping 35 cents. I never realized that they were good to eat, but why shouldn't squirrels be good to eat, I thought—after all, people do eat rabbits.

"Bob," Mom scolded dad again, "please don't put any more silly notions into his head. Bobby, your father is just fooling you. You know we don't eat squirrels."

"Mmm-mmm," Dad replied, smacking his lips. "Just the thought of a good feed of roasted squirrel makes me hungry all over."

"When are we gonna eat them, Dad?" I asked. I had never eaten squirrel, but just listening to Dad and watching him smack his lips, I knew they had to be good. Why, I could almost taste a good feed of roast squirrel myself.

"Well now, let me see," Dad replied. "Let's just put these little fellas right here, close to the stove and let them thaw out." He took the squirrels and laid them out in neat little rows in front of the cookstove.

"Are we gonna eat them, then, Dad?" I asked.

"We'll hafta wait, till they thaw out," he replied. "Then we're gonna skin them."

"Then can we cook up a mess and eat 'em?" I asked again.

"No, we can't," Mom replied angrily.

"Why not?" I asked.

"Because then we're going to throw them out," she replied. "They'll be outside where the birds can pick on them."

"But I wanna have a mess of squirrels," I protested.

"Mmm-mmm," Dad sighed and licked his chops. "I

tell you, there's nothing better than a good squirrel stew."

"Stew? Are we gonna have squirrel stew?" I asked. "I thought we was gonna have roast squirrel – tempting morsels."

"That's it! You're going to bed," Mom replied. "I've heard enough about squirrel for one night."

That was it. Final. When Mom decided that we were going to bed, we went to bed.

Larry, Gwen, and Judy quickly went to sleep. They didn't seem to care whether they had any squirrel, roasted, stewed, or otherwise. But not me. I knew that as soon as I went to sleep, Mom and Dad were going to have a mess of squirrel all to themselves.

Dad was humming happily as I snuck through the sheet for the umpteenth time. The squirrels had thawed, and Dad, now seated over by the cookstove, was busy skinning them and stretching their little hides. I knew that cooked squirrel was the next thing on their agenda.

I almost made it to Dad's chair before Mom intercepted me. Once more, she turned me around and marched me straight back through the sheets.

"You just want me to go to sleep so that you can eat all the squirrels by yourself!" I howled as she grabbed a handful of blankets and pulled them over me. I knew that the minute I went to sleep, Mom and Dad were going to gorge themselves on those squirrels . . . .

"Remember, Boy," Grandfather called over his shoulder, "you tell your mother I'll be around tomorrow night for some of her squirrel stew."

"Yeah, I'll tell her all right," I said as I watched Grandfather walk away chuckling to himself. "But she ain't gonna be happy."

You just wait, old man, I mumbled to myself, you just wait until I get a little bigger. I'm gonna learn how to cook and I'll make a real big ol' squirrel stew just for you and Dad, and you'll be eating it all right. Then we'll see who's laughing and who's smacking his lips.

TINY'S CHRISTMAS DINNER

I was one excited young man sitting in the passenger seat of the beat-up old International lumber truck. It was like trying to sit the saddle of a bucking bronc, I thought, as the latest bump in the road launched me towards the windshield. I glanced over at the driver, who was expertly manoeuvering his rig along the rough, narrow bush trail he referred to as the haul road. In places, the old truck dropped into holes that looked like craters; in other places, the truck bounced over big old spruce tree roots. I marvelled at his ability to inch the truck between trees where the opening appeared to be far too narrow. There were hairpin corners around huge trees, where I braced myself, waiting for the impact of metal on wood. Although many trees showed gaping wounds, the telltale signs of past encounters, there were none on this day.

Today, I considered myself very lucky, for I had been allowed to miss the last day of school before the start of the Christmas holidays. I was on my way to the bush camp where Dad worked.

"Boy, I'll bet Dad's really gonna be surprised to see me," I said to the driver as he cranked on the steering wheel. One thing I was quickly learning about bush-camp roads—anything more than thirty feet passed as a straight stretch.

"Yeah, you can say that again," chuckled the driver. "I can't wait to see old Bob's face when I tell him he's got company for the night. I imagine he'll be right happy with this little surprise, especially when he realizes you'll be sharing his bunk."

"Not me," I replied quickly. "I'll probably sleep on the floor."

I had often heard Dad say, "As soon as Bob's old enough, I'm going to take him to camp. He can be my swamper."

"He's not going to work in any bush camp!" Mom would reply angrily. "He's only ten! He's staying right here and going to school!" Mom had visions of greater things.

"You know, Florence, I finished school in grade three. Bob could be earning nine dollars a week right now," Dad stated solemnly.

"Wow," I had replied, "nine dollars a week." I looked at my brother Larry. He sat there looking back at me. I don't know what he was thinking. But I knew that nine dollars a week was a whole lot better than the nickel he and I were splitting for cutting, skidding, peeling, and creosoting telephone poles.

"You can forget about the bush camps," Mom

informed me in no uncertain terms. "You're going to finish school and get yourself a decent good-paying job."

Man, I often dreamed of working with Dad in the bush camps. During the summer months, the dreams were spurred to greater heights and glory when Dad and other loggers would joke and kid about their life in the bush camps. To me it sounded like the most wonderful life in the world. Working in the lumber camps was just the kind of life that an outdoor country boy like myself would really enjoy.

In my mind, I could plainly see myself working outside all day, from dawn to dusk, felling, limbing, bucking up, and skidding saw logs. At mealtimes, I would join the other men in the cookhouse. The table would be set, and heaps of food, steaming hot food prepared by the cook, would be placed on the table by the bullcook. Yes, I knew that all the loggers had their meals prepared for them by the camp cook, and they all ate together in a huge cookhouse. After a hearty supper, I could see myself leaning back and listening to Dad play the guitar. I had heard many a logger say that the best part of working in the bush was listening to Dad pickin' and singin' at the end of the day. But the best part for me would be no school and no girls.

As the truck wound its way along the haul road, I was picturing the logging camp in my mind. For I knew, in my mind, just how a logging camp would look: All the buildings would be like little cottages, snuggled comfortably under the trees. They would all be in a neat row, just like a small town. Each one would be painted a different colour. Ah yes, I thought as I bounced and bumped around in the cab of the old International truck, there was nothing that I didn't know about a logging camp.

I knew there had to be an end to that rough, winding haul road, and my butt prayed that it would come soon. The haul road seemed to snake endlessly through the forest of spruce and pine, and at times I felt that I would never reach that magical paradise I so often dreamed of.

Then I thought I could smell the woodsmoke from the chimneys at the camp, but as the old truck bounced, whined, and squeaked through the forest, I realized that it was only my imagination.

Suddenly, without any warning, the old truck crept around a stand of spruce trees, and right smack dab in the middle of the road was a little shack. I looked around and spotted other little shacks. Grubby, ugly little shacks. And there was junk. Junk scattered all over the place. It looked as if we had arrived at a garbage dump with a bunch of shacks around it.

"What's this?" I asked the driver.

"This, my boy, is the logging camp," he replied wearily. "And none too soon either, I might add." He stopped the old truck and shut off the engine. Then he stretched his arms and yawned.

"This! This is the logging camp?" I repeated. I couldn't begin to hide the disappointment in my voice.

"That's right," he answered. "This is the logging camp, Bobby. It's the end of the line. Let's get out and see where everybody is."

Slowly I looked around. Trees had been bulldozed to the sides of the clearing to make way for the camp. There were a half-dozen shacks. These were not cottages. In fact, I sort of hoped that they were not the bunkhouses. They were scattered around the small clearing, some of them shoved back between the trees. The buildings were constructed out of rough-sawn boards. So bare were the boards, that even one dab of paint would have looked out of place. A mist or smoke seemed to seep through the dingy little windows of a couple of the shacks. At others, the same stuff sifted through the cracks around the doors. I shuddered when I noticed that more mist or smoke was seeping through the cracks in the walls. This must be a different camp, I thought—certainly it was not the camp the loggers joked and kidded about.

"This can't be our camp. Whose camp is this?" I asked the driver.

"This here, this is our camp. It is the end of the line, Bobby my boy," he chuckled.

"Are you pullin' my leg?" I asked.

"This is it boy, home sweet home," he laughed.

"Where's my Dad?" I asked the truck driver.

"I don't rightly know," he replied and looked around the camp. "But since he won't be going home until tomorrow, I'd say he's most likely in his bunkhouse, cleaning up for supper."

"Which is his bunkhouse?" I asked.

"I don't know that either," he said. "I guess we'll just have to go and see if we can rustle him out, won't we? But first, I have to drain the rad." I waited while he dug a wrench out of the glovebox, then got out and crawled under the front of the truck. In a second, a stream of hot water and steam spurted out onto the packed snow.

"I'll bet Dad'll really be surprised to see me!" I sang out as I tramped along behind the driver. I was disappointed in the camp, but I was sure excited at the thought of seeing Dad. We walked over to the nearest bunkhouse and the driver yanked the door open.

"Bob Adams in here?" he called out.

"The catskinner's in the end bunkhouse," someone replied.

"Close the door. Yer lettin' in the winter," someone else bellowed.

I couldn't wait for the driver, so I ran ahead to the end bunkhouse and just as I had watched the truck driver do, I yanked open the door. A burst of hot air hit me, and a cloud of mist blotted out everything on the inside of the bunkhouse.

"Bob Adams in here?" I yelled as I stepped through the door. I had been right in my earlier thoughts—Dad certainly was surprised to see me. He was sitting on his bunk, picking away on the guitar, as I burst in. His head shot up and he looked at me like he had seen a ghost.

"What the—" he stammered. Then he slowly got up. He walked to the door and looked past me, outside. The only things that hadn't been there five minutes earlier were the lumber truck and the driver who was coming towards the bunkhouse.

"Bob?" he seemed to question my existence. "Where did you come from?"

"Hey, Bob, I brung you an early Christmas present," laughed the driver.

"Yeah, Dad, I came in the truck," I answered proudly as if I was a man of the world. "I come to go home with you tomorrow."

"Does your mother know you're here?" he asked.

"Yeah, an' she said I didn't hafta go to school today, 'cause I was comin' to get you to come home for Christmas," I informed him happily.

"I see," he replied, then took another look out the door. Dad just knew there had to be someone else out there, but there wasn't.

"It's okay, isn't it Dad?" I asked.

"I guess so," Dad responded. "As long as your mother knows." Dad didn't sound that certain about it though, and he still had a rather puzzled look on his face.

"C'mon in and shut the door, kid. You born in a barn or are you trying to heat up the countryside?" shouted one of the other men in the bunkhouse.

"Mom said I could eat in the cookshack with the men and I could sleep in the bunkhouse with you!" I exclaimed excitedly. Man, I was just bursting with pride to be in camp with Dad and in his bunkhouse.

"She did, did she!" He sort of chuckled, but Dad kept looking at the door, expecting that someone else was going to come in.

"And did your mother send you a bedroll?" he asked.

"Mom said not to worry," I replied. I turned and pulled the door shut behind me. It was then I noticed how dark it was inside. One little window at the end of the building was so dirty that it provided almost no light at all. The airtight heater, glowing red, in the middle of the room was belting out the heat, and it threw more light than the window. I made my way over to Dad's bunk. It was a single cot with a thin mattress and an even thinner blanket.

"This is a pretty narrow bed," I mentioned to Dad as I took a seat on the edge of it. One look around and I knew right away I wasn't going to be sleeping on the floor. "Do you think we're both gonna fit on this thing?"

"Well, let's see," Dad replied, looking first at me and then at the bed. Usually when a man comes into camp, he brings a bedroll with him and he sleeps on the floor. Now, if you didn't bring a bedroll with you, then you have to either sleep on the floor with nothing, or with me. If you want to sleep with me, I guess we'll just have to make do."

"Mom said I could eat in the cookshack, with the loggers," I quickly blurted out. I didn't want him to forget the eating part. My imagination had run rampant all the way from Edson, and I couldn't wait to get a taste of camp food. Just the very thought of them tasty morsels that loggers ate made my mouth water.

"Well, you certainly picked a good night for it," Dad smiled. "Most of the boys will be leaving camp either tonight or in the morning, and the cook has rustled us up a Christmas dinner. You better take your coat off and sit back and relax a spell. It'll be a while before we eat."

I took off my coat and leaned back against the rough boards, settling myself between a couple of the 2x4 studs. They served as both the outside and inside walls. Even though it was stifling hot in that small shack, the cold of winter could be felt right through the boards. I quickly grabbed my coat and put it between me and the boards. The fire roared in the red-hot airtight heater, and the lid was bouncing up and down. *Whump, whump, whump.* It sounded like a metal drum.

Dad picked up his guitar again and started picking.

"Jingle bells, jingle bells," he sang out as the festive spirit set in. Other men walked in, and soon the bunkhouse was full of loggers. They all joined in and were singing Christmas songs. I opened my mouth and warbled along. I was the one singing out of key.

"Tiny been in here?" asked a man who suddenly appeared through the mist at the door. Most everybody shook their heads.

"Nope. He's not in here. Haven't seen him all afternoon," someone replied. "What's old Tiny up to anyway?"

"Don't know. Last we saw of him, he was down at the barn muckin' around with the horses. Tellin' 'em his tale of woe. Now we can't find him anywhere."

"We'll tell him you're lookin' for him if he shows up," laughed another.

"Well, if he shows up, I'd tread softly if I were you," cautioned the man. "Old Tiny's had himself a snootful and he's got the blues. He's feelin' a little sorry for himself. He's cussin' and moanin' about not gettin' home for Christmas agin this year. Tiny says it's bin many a year since he's seen his family, an' he doesn't even know if he has a home to go to any more. He's in a pretty ugly mood right now. You boys better walk softly if he shows up."

"Who's Tiny?" I whispered to Dad.

"He's one of the loggers," Dad answered. "They say he comes from down east somewhere. Every Christmas he ties one on and gets real blubbery for a couple of days."

"How come that man said to walk softly?"

"Tiny's got a short fuse, and it's best to stay out of his way." Dad smiled. "Sometimes, he can be a little tough to deal with."

"We'll keep an eye peeled for him," someone called out. The man searching for Tiny stepped back outside. The door closed. It was getting late. Once more, in the glow of the airtight heater, Dad began to pick his guitar, and the men returned to their singing.

It was a pretty exciting start to the Christmas holidays, sitting with the loggers in my Dad's bunkhouse, while Dad picked his guitar and led the singsong. Dad knew every song, and he could play anything that he was asked. In the cheery atmosphere of the dimly lit bunkhouse, I soon forgot about the rough road, the disappointing camp site, and Tiny. Even though the sweat was pouring off me, I snuggled in as close as I could get to Dad. I was in a world of my own that afternoon. I knew some of the words to the tunes that Dad played, but whether I knew the words or not, I belted out one song after the other. This was the life, I thought. There was no doubt, I was one of the men. I was destined to be a logger. The afternoon flew by.

The loggers were a relaxed lot, but when that bell sounded, calling them for supper, I was glad I was sitting on Dad's bunk. Man, those loggers peeled out of there as if the place was on fire. Dad set his guitar on the bunk, and we, too, started for the cookshack.

"Listen, Bob," Dad said as we neared the cookshack. "I want you to remember something, son."

"Yeah?" I replied.

"There are rules here, and one of them is that there's no talking in the cookshack during the meal, except to ask someone to pass you something. Do you understand that?"

"How come you can't talk?" I asked, thinking of all the chatter that went on around our table back in Edson.

"That's just the way it is in bush camps," he replied. "It's one of the rules. No talking at the table. Now, you remember what I told you, son."

"I'll remember, Dad," I spouted confidently. "You can count on me, I'll remember."

"Oh no. For the love of Pete!" I heard someone ahead of me exclaim as he walked through the door.

"What's the matter, Dad?" I asked trying to see ahead of me, but my vision was blocked by the loggers in front. "I thought there was no talking in the cookshack," I added.

"I don't know," Dad replied. "Just remember what I told you. No talking." There was an eerie silence, broken only by a slurred voice.

"Merry Christmas," blubbered the voice repeatedly.

"Merry Christmas." I was walking right in front of Dad, and I felt his fingers bite into my shoulders as we entered the cookshack. Standing just inside the door was a mountain of a man.

"That's Tiny," Dad whispered.

As the man who had been looking for Tiny earlier had said, Tiny had had a snootful. The big man had somehow got into the cookshack before anyone else and was standing at the end of one table. On the table in front of him was a washtub. I watched as each logger picked up a plate. One by one, they walked over to Tiny. Some hesitated, but all held out their plate. Tiny was serving the loggers their Christmas dinner.

It appeared that Tiny had decided to bypass a few of the serving steps. Yes, Tiny had taken the entire dinner—turkey, mashed spuds, turnips, carrots, cranberries, gravy, Christmas cake, and pie—and he had dumped the whole works into the tub.

"Merry Christmas!" wailed the big man as tears streamed down his cheeks. I saw him drive those massive paws into the tub, cup them together, and scoop out dinner and dessert. Not so carefully, Tiny deposited a huge gob of the offering onto each plate. It was a gut-wrenching mixture, but dinner was served. No two loggers got the same plateful. Every helping was different, every helping an adventure. And, with every helping, Tiny would mutter, "Merry Christmas."

"Merry Christmas, Tiny," each logger replied in a whisper as they accepted their meal and walked silently past. Each took a seat at the table and commenced eating without uttering a single word.

My eyes were as big as saucers and my mouth hung open as I watched Tiny scoop my meal out of the tub. I stared at his massive hands and his big, hairy arms. Everything seemed to be clinging to the hair on his arms, there were gobs of spuds and gravy and bits of cake and . . . and probably horse poop, I thought. My imagination was running wild, thinking of what might be hidden under the covering of food. Oh man, I hoped that Tiny had washed his hands after mucking around with the horses. My hands were shaking and my knees were knocking when Tiny had scraped the last bit of food (at least I hoped it was all food) off his hands and onto my plate.

"Merry Christmas, boy!" Tiny bawled amid a new flood of tears. Then to add to my fears, he reached over and patted my head with a huge, gooey, gobby paw. I could feel what I hoped was only spuds, gravy, and cranberries being ground into my hair.

"M-M-Merry Christmas, M-M-Mister Tiny," I stammered, scared that I would say something that would upset him. Man, he's a giant, I thought as I stood in front of him.

I bent forward to get a better look at Tiny's hands, but I felt Dad nudging me along. Dad motioned to a place at the table and I sat down. Dad was right, I thought, looking around the table. No one was speaking, and there was no need to ask anyone to pass anything. Tiny had delivered it all, all at once.

I noticed that the guy across from me had what looked like half the turkey on his plate. He was munching away, happily. I looked down at the soupy mix that had dripped off my plate and onto the table. I had a smattering of carrots, spuds, turnips, and gravy, but there was no turkey swimming in the mess on my plate. I noticed I had a very dark, clear, thin gravy. It was certainly not anything like the gravy that Mom made when she cooked a turkey. Then I noticed a piece of something else wedged into the spuds.

"What is this stuff?" I whispered to Dad as I stared at the concoction on my plate.

"That's Tiny's Christmas dinner," whispered the guy sitting across the table with half the turkey. "Shut up and eat it, kid."

"Who's talking?" boomed a mighty voice that shook the cookshack. I looked around the table and every head was down. The men were shovelling food into their faces as fast as they could.

"Here, you want some more, kid?" Tiny roared again. He charged across the room like a raging bull, goop dripping from his hands. He flung another handful onto my plate. Spuds and gravy splashed across the table. No one moved. I was shaking like a leaf, I was so scared. Then I remembered Dad's warning: "No talking, unless you're asking someone to pass something." Unless I wanted to eat that whole tubful, I knew that I'd better keep my mouth shut.

I joined the rest of the men at the table and shovelled in a spoonful of the concoction that strongly resembled the swill that Grandfather fed his hogs. Instantly my stomach rebelled. I gagged and retched as I tasted the first mouthful.

"Oh no," I moaned silently. "It tastes like . . . like

coffee. It is, it's coffee, not gravy. No wonder it looked like such runny gravy," I thought. The second and the third mouthfuls also tasted like coffee. Tiny had dumped the coffee into the tub as well. I swallowed hard, trying to keep everything down. The chunk of stuff wedged into the mashed spuds had once been Christmas cake, but it also tasted like coffee. I had only sneaked a taste of coffee once and decided I wasn't missing much. For the first time in my life, I didn't go back for a second helping of Christmas dinner—but then, I noticed, neither had anyone else.

Finally, supper was over and, like everyone else, I had choked down the last of the slop. I felt sick to my stomach. I thought for sure I was going to barf. Man, was I happy when I got out of that cookshack. I had been dreading the thought of walking past Tiny with my plate. I was sure he would plop another gob of the goo on my plate and I would have to eat it. But he ignored me and my goop-covered hair.

I began to feel a little better once I got out into the cold winter air. I followed after Dad as he hurried towards the bunkhouse. In the doorway to the bunkhouse, I was hit with a blast of hot air from the airtight heater. Suddenly, I felt this urge to barf again.

"I gotta go to bed," I muttered, and I started to get undressed.

"You might want to consider leaving your clothes on," Dad mentioned as if it was no big deal. "It's gonna get a bit cool in here before morning." I didn't argue. I pulled my pants back up and crawled onto Dad's bunk. I felt so rotten, I just wanted to die.

It was obvious, once Dad crawled into the bunk, that there was not a whole lot of room. The blanket felt heavy and hot, and the cot was far too small. Soon I was squished up against the wall. I could feel every 2x4 on my back.

I had a tough time sleeping. Soon every logger in the room, except me, was snoring, sawing logs like crazy. The airtight heater was still red-hot, and the lid was bouncing like crazy. *Whump, whump, whump.* It pounded into the night. Man, but it was stiflingly hot. I was suffocating. I couldn't sleep and I knew that at any minute I was going to be sick. I was going to die out in this god-forsaken place, and no one would even notice. I threw off the blanket. I had to cool down. I pushed and shoved at Dad. I tried to get as far away from him as I could. I needed some space, some cool air.

It wasn't long before I got my wish. The wood in the heater burned down. The red glow died away and the fire went out. Instantly, the cool air from the great outdoors began to creep into the bunkhouse. I was getting my wish, it was begining to cool off.

In fact, it cooled off too fast and it got darned cold in there. That bunkhouse went from sweat box to freezing cold in minutes. Frost poured through the single layer of boards. I pulled the blanket over me. The blanket that only a few minutes earlier had been hot and heavy was now cold and thin. Pretty soon, I was shivering like crazy, and my teeth were chattering like a handful of Chiclets. I pulled the blanket over my head. Man, it felt colder inside the bunkhouse than it was outside.

Now I felt sick, I felt clammy, and I was freezing to

death. I crowded into Dad, seeking some warmth, and cursed the blanket for being so thin and the cot for being so large.

I lay awake most of the night, not from the excitement and anticipation that I had felt when I came into camp. No, I lay awake because I was scared that if I went to sleep, I would never wake up. I knew I was going to freeze to death.

"C'mon Bob, let's go and get us some breakfast," Dad called, his voice singing out in the darkness. I opened my eyes. I guess I must have dozed off. What a relief, to find that I was still alive and the inside of the bunkhouse was once again warm. Someone had lit the airtight heater, and once more the lid was bouncing. *Whump, whump, whump,* it banged in the darkness.

Slowly, I crawled out of Dad's bunk. I was dreading the thought of returning to the cookshack. After last night, I knew I couldn't take Tiny's Christmas breakfast.

Tiny was gone from the cookshack, so I loaded up my plate with a generous helping of bacon, eggs, and pancakes. I sat down at the table. Except for the sound of cutlery on the plates, the room was deathly silent. Then I got a good whiff of the coffee. That stopped me—it turned my stomach and made me retch.

The truck was loaded when Dad and I left the cookshack. It was time to go home. The truck's passenger load had increased. Besides myself and the driver, Dad and two other loggers were crammed into the cab. I got the seat on Dad's lap. Even though I was a big kid, big enough that Dad thought I was old enough to work in the bush camp, I found a great deal of comfort sitting on his lap. As the truck wound its way back through the timber, bouncing and swerving along the narrow haul road, I snuggled up on Dad's lap and I slept.

Somewhere, my trip to the bush camp had lost its lustre, and I had lost my enthusiasm to be a logger. Oh no, the life of a logger was not for me.

THE THREE-MILE McLEOD

Dozens of us were strung out in a long line through the forest. Since dawn, we had been slowly, methodically, searching every clump of brush, every tuft of grass, and looking under every deadfall. The sun was almost directly overhead now. It was getting close to noon.

It seemed like forever, but it was only yesterday when I had phoned my biology teacher and begged to be excused from the final exam. A child was lost. The RCMP had asked for volunteers to join in the search.

I and two friends were excused from writing the exam.

I looked up through the pines at the sun. Yeah, I thought, it's close to noon all right. I wondered how my classmates were doing. I figured the biology exam would almost be over by now. Man, but I wished I was back at school, sitting in my classroom, writing that exam, and the little person we were searching for was safe at home. That would have meant that our search had been successful. But it had not been. Not so far, anyway. Standing around staring up at the sky was not going to help if that little person was ever going to get a chance to write an exam. I shook my head, then plunged back into the thicket with renewed determination.

The cool of the morning had long since passed, and it was now a hot and humid day. Beads of sweat stood out on my forehead before joining forces and streaming down my face. I looked down at my clothes, dirty and wet, wringing wet with sweat. They clung to my body like rags. Earlier in the morning, they had been dry—wrinkled and slept-in, but dry. We had searched until dark the previous day, and the three of us had spent the night in the car so that we could get an early start.

After several fruitless hours of walking, crawling, and searching, I emerged from the brush and stood above the river. From the bank, high above the water, I looked down at the sandy shore and the peaceful water. I was exhausted and dejected. I plunked myself down, dangling my feet over the edge. Below me in the sand, there were tracks, many tracks. I was not the first one to arrive.

I stared down into the tranquil water slowly flowing by. Here, the river was wide, the current not very strong. It was calm, serene, a peaceful country scene. It looked like the perfect place for swimming, but rivers, I had already learned, could be very deceiving. Watching the water, my mind wandered, reflecting on days gone by. Hot summer days. Four little kids. The South Road. The McLeod River. The three-mile McLeod, our swimming hole. It seemed like only yesterday . . . .

"Now, don't forget, I want you home in time for supper, and don't forget you have chores to do when you get home." It was Mom's constant reminder whenever we kids headed for the three-mile McLeod to spend a day on the beach. We would take a picnic lunch. We would play, eat, and "swim—" although not one of us could swim a stroke if we had to, we would all give it a try in the cold, cold waters.

"Don't worry, Mom," I warbled. "I'll take care of them. We'll be home in plenty of time for chores and supper."

"Bobby," Mom's voice was loud and clear as she lectured me. "Remember, now, you're the oldest, the man of the house. You make sure you watch out for your brother and sisters. And please be careful."

"I know, Mom," I replied. "I know. You don't have to tell me the same thing every time."

"I'll tell you every time, and you better make sure you listen every time," she stated emphatically.

"I know, I know," I replied, exasperated. "It just wastes time, Mom. If you didn't have to tell us all the time, we could almost be at the swimmin' hole by now, you know." At ten, I was the oldest, and Judy, the youngest, was five. Being the oldest, it was expected that I would look after my siblings, and I accepted the responsibility.

Carrying syrup pails containing the picnic lunch Mom had packed for us, we trailed out of the yard and turned right, heading south toward the river. There had been no rain on the South Road for several days. The normally hard-packed clay surface had been ground to a fine powder. The entire road was covered with a heavy layer of powdery dust. The worst area was the small knoll just south of our farm. Here, the powder lay like spilled sacks of flour, several inches thick. The pine and spruce trees on either side of the road were covered with a thick coating of powdery clay. The trees, the grass, everything along the South Road, had long since lost its colour. Everything was the colour of clay. It seemed as if there was no happy medium on the South Road. When the weather was hot and dry, the road was a dust bowl. When it rained, the road was a sea of mud.

We hadn't gone far, only to the first knoll south of the house—the dustiest place on earth—when a car roared past us. Thick dust billowed up in its wake. The dust was so thick it blotted out the sun, engulfing us, choking us. We huddled at the side of the road. We covered our faces with our towels and squeezed our eyes tight. There was no breeze to carry the dust one way or the other. We knew from past experience that dust would hang over the South Road like a low cloud long after the vehicle had passed. It would stay, it seemed, forever suspended.

"I knew we should have left earlier," I grumbled. "If Mom hadn't of yakked so long, we would have been there by now. Now we're gonna hafta eat dust all the way."

At Bench Creek we took a break from the dust and our walking. Larry and I threw clumps of clay at the large dragonflies that flitted over the water.

"Hey, look at this, Rob," Larry called out. He pointed to the clear water under the bridge.

I walked over and peered down, into the shadows under the bridge. Then I saw it—the sleek body, with a huge dorsal fin. An Arctic grayling. Back and forth it darted, picking up bits of food the current swept its way.

"You got any snarin' wire with you?" I asked Larry.

"No. It's at home in my fishing bag," he replied.

"Mine too," I cursed. "Man, just look at him, beggin' to be caught. Look, see—he always returns to the same spot. I could snare him easily, right here, from the top of the bridge."

"Yeah," Larry replied. "So could I, and I saw him first."

"Ah, man," I cursed. "Where is a guy's snare pole when he needs it?" We both just stood there helplessly on the bridge, looking longingly at a sure meal swimming right under our noses.

Past Sliva's dairy farm we walked, turning east at the country lane, a trail between two fields, that went all the way to the river. We were almost at the swimming hole now, away from the dusty road. The lane, dotted with the odd poplar tree, was very picturesque and could easily have been the setting for a calendar picture. At the end of the lane, we followed a trail down the steep embankment, not paying any attention to the steps that someone had painstakingly dug out of the dirt and rock. We raced through the chokecherry trees that grew along the trail, forming a canopy of leaves and branches overhead that blocked out the sun. Their limbs hung heavy with berries not yet ripened. Finally, we arrived at the short, narrow strip of sand on the banks of the McLeod River, our beach.

"Last one in's a rotten egg!" someone yelled. We grabbed our bathing suits and ran into the bush to change. Boys on one side of the path, girls on the other. Out of the bush we charged, screaming and yelling, into the water.

The river was wide, the water calm and peaceful. But all was not what it appeared to be, for not far from the shore, the water got deep and flowed faster. We would stay in the shallow water. At least—as the oldest, the man of the house when Dad was away—I was supposed to make sure we stayed in the shallow water.

The cold water felt good after the long, hot walk. It felt good to get the layer of dust washed from my body. Splashing in the water was not only hard work on a hot summer day, it was darned cold work. The cold water worked its magic, and before long we were transformed from hot dusty little kids to cold clean little kids. In the frigid waters of the McLeod River, our lips turned blue. We shivered like crazy and sported goose pimples the size of chokecherries. It was not long before we retired, four shivering popsicles with legs, to the warmth of the sun and sand. It was time for a much-needed picnic lunch.

After lunch, however, it was time for adventure. At ten years old, I was not content to stay and play in the sand and splash in the shallow water. I wanted to explore. I surveyed the object of many a dream—the opposite bank of the three-mile McLeod. I eyeballed the cliffs, and the hordes of swallows that darted and flitted from their nests, neat little round holes dug into the steep banks. I eyeballed sand, far better sand than we were playing on. I eyeballed the far side of the river.

Larry and I had often talked about getting to the other side. We had even made some plans for what we would do over there. And we had almost made it over to the other side once . . . .

One day, Larry and I each hauled an old inner tube down the dusty road to the swimming hole, and we made our move. In the shallow water, we climbed aboard our inner tubes and, like true adventurers, we started paddling with our hands. We were headed for the far side of the river, for the cliffs, the swallows, and the better sand. With the tire tubes, the McLeod was ours to conquer.

"Hey Rob, we should have thought of this earlier. This is easy." Larry warbled. He was paddling leisurely as we moved toward the middle of the river.

"You can say that again," I replied. I looked back to see where Gwen and Judy were, so that I could judge how far we had come . . . but they weren't there. The swimming hole wasn't there. Everything was way back up the river. I looked downstream, way down to where the rapids were. But the rapids weren't way down the river. They were getting pretty close, close enough to hear.

"We better turn back," I yelled. "We're almost in the rapids!" I didn't need to yell again. Both Larry and I were stroking our arms, paddling like crazy.

The closer we got to the rapids, the faster the McLeod River flowed. As we neared the safety of the bank, way downstream from where we started, I was paddling like a wild man. In fact, I paddled so hard that my inner tube ran right up on top of Larry's. I could tell by the look in his eyes that he was surprised. He just couldn't believe how fast I could paddle. As my tube slid up over his tube, Larry's eyes bugged out and his mouth popped open. If I thought he was surprised before, that was nothing compared to the look on his face as his tube dipped and he flipped right into the frigid waters.

Suddenly, there was only an empty rubber tube bobbing around on the river. Larry had disappeared. He just slipped under the water, under his tube. Down he went, into the depths of the McLeod River.

Now, I had always known that Larry was a fighter, but boy, did he ever surprise me. I didn't even know that he could swim. He hadn't been down long when he reappeared. He shot up to the surface and popped out of the water like a cork. His mouth was closed, but his eyes were even buggier than when he went in. They looked like giant marbles. His feet were kicking wildly, and his arms were flapping around like a couple of socks in the wind. His fingers grabbed frantically for something, anything, to hold onto.

It was a good thing for Larry that we were close to the shore when he finally got a grip on his inner tube. He splashed and thrashed his way the last few feet and finally pulled himself ashore just short of the rapids. I don't think Larry was too happy with me.

"What do you think you're doing?" he growled at me. "You just about drownded me!"

"Did not," I mumbled. "It's not my fault you fell off your stupid tube."

"You did too," he replied accusingly. "You knocked me off my tube."

"Did not," I said. "Anyway, how could you drown when you could swim? I didn't know you could swim."

"I can't swim," he mumbled. "But I can open my eyes under water."

"No you can't," I challenged him. There was no way he could open his eyes under water. I was older than he was and I couldn't open my eyes under water.

"Yes I can," he replied happily. "That was the first time I opened my eyes under water, and they stayed open the whole time."

Well, I couldn't argue with that. After all, I had seen his eyes, two giant marbles, wide open when he went in and even wider open when he came out. Grudgingly, I had to concede that Larry probably could open his eyes under water.

That night, Gwen told Mom of our little misadventure. Mom was less than impressed with our adventurous spirit. That was almost the end of our swimming. It was definitely the end of our adventures with the rubber tubes . . . .

So here, we were at the swimming hole, with the far side of the river beckoning to me . . . the banks, the swallows, the sand . . .

"Bob!" They all called my name. "Come over here. It's better over here. There's more of everything."

It wasn't that far, I thought. Today would be as good a day as any to sample the other side. Why not? But I needed someone to go with me. I needed some moral and physical support. I needed Gwen—that way, she couldn't tell Mom.

"We should cross the river," I casually mentioned to Gwen. "It looks like there's more sand over there." I pointed to the high banks of beautiful sand on the far side.

"We're not supposed to leave the swimming hole," Gwen informed me. "And remember, Mom said you're supposed to stay right here." I ignored her warnings.

"We can walk across the river down at the rapids," I said very knowledgeably.

"You can not," she said. But after thinking about it for a second, she added, "Can you?"

Aha, I chuckled to myself. I've got her.

"You sure can," I said, quite seriously. "Do you want me to show you?"

"No, I don't. How do you know you can walk across?" she asked. "You've never done that."

"I have too," I responded. "I've walked across down

there lots of times." I nodded my head up and down a few times.

"You have not."

"Yes, I have too," I boasted. "If you're too chicken, I'll show you how it's done." I got up and headed downstream towards the rapids. Actually, I had never walked across the river, but I had heard some of the bigger boys say you could walk across just about where the rapids start. I felt confident that if they could do it, so could I.

Lunch buckets and towels were left on the beach as we trailed along the river-bank, downstream towards the rapids.

"Here it is," I said when we arrived at the head of the rapids. I could clearly see the rocks under the water. It didn't look very deep to me. This had to be the spot.

"This is where we start. Are you coming with me?"

Gwen grumbled, but then, reluctantly, she grabbed my hand and stepped into the river behind me. She was coming, but she was going to be holding onto something.

There was no sandy bottom here, only rocks—large rocks, small rocks, flat rocks, sharp rocks, and slippery rocks. Each step had to be carefully taken. Deeper into the river we moved, slowly, cautiously, testing each step. I was surprised at how much stronger the current was here than at the swimming hole. We had to brace ourselves to keep from being swept away. Every time I stopped, I could hear the far side of the river calling: the sand, the high banks, the swallows. Gwen clutched my hand tighter and, together, we continued. Once more,

I was about to conquer the McLeod River. But it was not as easy as I had thought, and the deeper the water got, the faster it flowed.

"I can't stand up," Gwen complained when the water got about chest-high. "The water keeps pushing my feet off the rocks. I want to go back."

"We can't go back now. Look, we're just about there," I mumbled, trying to sound encouraging. However, when I looked over at the far bank, it seemed to be getting farther away instead of closer.

"I don't care. I'm scared," she wailed. "I'm scared and I want to go back. Now!" I think she tried to stomp her foot, because at that moment, the current swept her up. Her grip tightened on my hand as her feet left the rocks on the bottom of the river. Like a shot, Gwen's feet and body were swept downstream, down towards the rapids.

Boy, what a dumb girl-trick to pull. She's just lucky I'm holding onto her, I thought as she disappeared under the water. I braced myself, and, with all my strength, I pulled her back towards me.

I hadn't counted on her next move, though. Fighting to regain her footing and thrashing about wildly, grabbing for anything to hang onto, she suddenly grasped my ankle with her free hand and yanked. In a second, my foot, too, left the dubious security of the slippery rocks. Then the other foot followed. In a flash, both Gwen and I were headed downstream, rolling with the current. Neither of us had a foot on the bottom. Frantically, we both struggled in the swift water. Then, by the grace of God, for it was certainly not due to any skill on my part, my free foot came up against a large rock. I braced myself, and the strength of the flow lifted my body up out of the water. I was able to haul a gasping, sputtering Gwen to her feet. We both regained our footing and stood shivering, up to our necks in really fast-flowing water. I don't know about Gwen, but I was scared to death.

"I hope you're satisfied," I grumbled. "You just about drowned both of us."

"I just about drowned us? *You* just about drowned us," she sputtered.

"Did not," I protested. "It was all your fault."

"Good! That'll teach you for talking me into this. I want to go back to shore right now!" she demanded. "I'm scared."

"Okay, then go back," I snapped at her. "I'll go across by myself."

"I can't get back by myself!" she howled and started to cry. "You got me into this and you can get me out, or I'm telling Mom on you. I'm scared and I want to go home. Anyway, I can hardly stand up because the water keeps pushing my feet off the rocks."

Grudgingly, I had to admit that it was getting difficult to stand, and I finally agreed to take her back to shore. For some reason, the excitement and anticipation of reaching the far side of the river were gone. They had slipped away a few seconds earlier. We were deeper into the rapids than I had planned to be, and I had to admit that I didn't really know which way to go. Neck-deep in the rapids, we started. We inched our way back, slipping and sliding and scared out of our wits.

"If I could swim, I'd go over there myself," I grumbled as we walked back along the riverbank towards the swimming hole.

"If you could swim, you wouldn't have tried to wade over to the other side and you wouldn't have tried to drown me," Gwen shot back.

No one talked about our little adventure as we left the river later in the afternoon. The four Adams kids walked home, together, just as we had done so many times before. Nothing had changed. There was not a breath of air. The South Road was just as dusty as we had left it earlier that day. The fine dust hung in the air. The grayling was still under the bridge, still waiting to be caught.

"I'm going to go home and get my snare wire and come back here and catch him for supper," I said.

"I'm coming with you," Larry piped up.

"I'm not going anywhere with you," Gwen snorted, giving me a dirty look and letting me know that she had neither forgotten nor forgiven me for our earlier adventure . . . .

"Let's go, guys," a voice boomed from along the riverbank, jarring me back to reality. "Time's a-wastin'. We're going to retrace our steps and work this patch of bush again. Let's be very thorough. We have to look under and into everything. If you've looked under a log or into a clump of brush once, do it again. Let's go, and keep the person on your right in sight at all times."

I shook my head and shuddered as I stood up. Once more, I thought of that day and the many other days that we four Adams kids had spent swimming in the McLeod River. It was a great place to spend a hot summer's day – a welcome relief from the sun, the flies, and the chores. It was the place where I eventually learned to swim. A place of many adventures, of many memories. But it was a dangerous place for four small kids and it was a miracle that any of us survived to remember those days.

I turned and walked back into the bush, praying. I prayed that our search would be successful.

It would be several days before I learned the fate of the child. A child whose adventure with the river had not ended as fortunately as ours.

THE PRINCESS

A real live princess, coming to Edson?

That was something beyond the wildest imagination of a kid living on the Stump Farm. It was impossible. Beyond comprehension. Viewed from our world, the real world, princesses were beautiful creatures who existed only in fairy tales. They were never very smart, because they were always eating poisoned apples or having a curse put on them. Fortunately, there was always a handsome young prince who just happened to be riding by on a magnificent stallion. The prince would gallop to the rescue, plant a tender kiss on the princess, and they would both live happily ever after. Princesses and princes didn't exist in our world. Nor, for that matter, did magnificent stallions. Not in 1951, in Edson, Alberta.

Then, one day, the impossible was possible. The biggest thing ever to occur in Edson was going to happen, and word spread like wildfire. A real live princess was indeed coming. I couldn't believe my ears when I heard the news. And, if a princess coming to Edson wasn't enough, the news got even better: The Edson Cadet Corps Drum and Bugle Band was going to march and play for the Princess. Bobby Adams was going to blow his bugle for a real live princess. Yes siree, I was going to be at the CNR station, right next to the Beanery, to celebrate the occasion. I would be the cock-o'-the-walk, envied by all. I was so excited the day I found out, I could hardly contain myself. Man, I ran all the way home to tell Mom the good news.

"Guess what, Mom!" I yelled as I charged into the house.

"I'm too tired to guess," Mom replied. She was busy getting supper ready and never stopped what she was doing. Never moved away from the cookstove.

"Guess!" I warbled again. I was so excited, I was just bursting.

"Please, Bobby, I'm very tired," Mom answered. "Why don't you just tell me?"

"The Princess is coming!" I blurted out. "She's coming here, to Edson."

Mom stopped and looked at me. She stood there for a long time and just looked at me. Mom did not seem to be nearly as impressed as I was. Then she finally spoke.

"What princess?" she asked.

"The Princess . . . the real Princess. Honest, Mom, she's coming . . . right here to Edson . . . this fall. And guess what, Mom!"

"What now?" she asked.

"I'm going to play my bugle for her."

"Bobby, Bobby, Bobby," Mom said. Mom sounded really tired. "You have such a vivid imagination. Who fills your head with this nonsense?"

"It's not nonsense, Mom," I assured her. "Honestly, Mom. They told us at band practice tonight. The Princess is coming to Edson, and we'll be marching down at the station. We're gonna be standin' right beside the Beanery where we can see everything. And we're gonna play."

"You're not just saying this, are you?" Mom asked. "You're serious."

"You bet!" I warbled happily. "An' . . . an' I hafta make sure my bugle is polished up so that the instructor can see his face in it."

"Can you imagine that," Mom said softly. This was too much for her, and she slowly sat down on a chair. "Can you imagine that. Do you know which one, Bobby? There's more than one princess, you know. Is it Princess Elizabeth? Oh please, Bobby, please tell me it's Princess Elizabeth. She's the most gorgeous creature in the world."

"Yeah. Yeah, I think that's her name. She is a princess, isn't she?" I asked.

"Oh, she is, Bobby, she is. She's a princess and she's beautiful," Mom cooed. "Oh my, Princess Elizabeth!"

Boy, Mom was sure getting excited. She didn't believe me when I first told her, but she was believing me now. Suddenly Mom didn't look tired anymore. Mom was in a dream, on another planet. She sat for a long time with a faraway look on her face.

Then, Mom jumped up and gave me a big hug.

"Oh, Bobby, I hope you're right."

I think Mom really liked the Princess. I think she even liked the whole Royal Family, whoever they were. I know every time I was around and someone mentioned them, her voice would get soft and mellow and she'd look off into the distance. Mom was looking off into the distance now. Her eyes were warm and misty and she had a soft smile on her face. She was happy. I liked it whenever Mom was happy, and right now she was really happy. I wished a princess would come to Edson every day.

"Can I go, Mom?" I asked. I just couldn't believe my good luck.

"To see the Princess?" Mom asked.

"Yeah. Can I go and see the Princess and play my bugle?"

"Well, of course you can. There's nothing in the world that could keep you away," Mom replied. "Why would you ask such a question?"

"Because the instructor said this was special, and we had to have our parents' permission. That's why."

"A team of wild horses couldn't keep you away," Mom smiled. "Or me either."

"Even if it's a school day, Mom?" I added.

"Even if it's a school day. It doesn't matter what day it is," she replied.

The whole town was abuzz with the excitement of the big event. The Royal Visit was on the lips of people everywhere. It was all they seemed to talk about. Since the end of World War II, this was certainly the biggest news to hit Edson, and no one seemed to miss an opportunity to talk about it. I know I didn't. I made sure I told everyone I talked to.

"You watch," I would toot to anyone and everyone who would listen. "I'll be blowing my horn for the Princess when that train pulls into the station. You'll see, I'll be in the front row of the bugle section."

A lot of things had changed since my first year in the Edson Cadet Corps Drum and Bugle Band. How could I ever forget marching up Main Street on July 1st, in my first Dominion Day parade. Mom said everyone was out of step, everyone, but me. I marched so well I had to march alone at the back of the troop. My bugle-playing, however, was not on par with my marching abilities, and I was strongly encouraged by the instructor to only pretend to blow my bugle.

Now things were different. My bugle-playing had improved considerably over the past couple of years. Not only did I know the notes – now I could play them. Yes, me and my bugle, we could make the sweetest sounds one man ever told another about.

As my bugle-playing improved, so had the marching abilities of many of the other boys in the cadet corps. Now when we marched and played, those clods who used to bump into me were actually able to march in a straight line. I noticed that they had got particularly good at turning the corners. No longer did a night of practice seem like running the gauntlet. As a result of these improvements, I had moved up in the corps. I now marched in the front of the bugle section, right behind the drummers, where, I could keep an eye on the majorettes, those pretty girls with the short skirts and the twirling batons. Yes, being in the Drum and Bugle Band was an exciting and rewarding experience.

But now, now that the Princess was coming, band practice had taken on a whole new dimension. There was electricity in the air. There was excitement. There was enthusiasm. Now the reward was even greater. Now we, the buglers, were going to blow our little heads off. We were going to play for the Princess.

I can tell you that I took my role very seriously. On evenings when there was a practice, I would run home from school, rush through my chores, wolf down my supper, and get into my uniform. Then I would pick up my trusty bugle and march out the door. All the way along the South Road I would practise marching and blowing. At the old bachelor Hubert's place, I would lift the bugle to my lips and let fly with a little refrain. He would come to the door and wave.

"Nice noise, Bobby," he would call out. "You must keep practising." I don't think old Hubert had much of an ear for music.

But Nick-the-Dog-Man's dogs did. In the distance, I could hear them joining in.

Aaarrroooowwwwww, howled the dogs.

As I marched past Ma and Grandfather's house, I let them know that I was on my way to practise for the Princess. They, too, had the pleasure of enjoying my talents with the bugle. By this time, Nick-the-Dog-Man's dogs were howling up a storm, and they were scaring the dickens out of Grandfather's hogs.

However, past Grandfather's place it was a different

story. As soon as I'd finished giving Ma and Grandfather a good toot, I tucked my bugle under my arm and very cautiously tippytoed past Nick-the-Dog-Man's place. He would have to get along without the benefit of my talents. Blowing the bugle from a distance was one thing, but there was no way I was going to tempt those dogs up close.

Past Nick-the-Dog-Man's place, at the top of the rise, I would do a snappy about-turn. Then, once again, I'd hoist my bugle. I'd play a long, defiant note. Instantly, those dogs howled and wailed. Both the dogs and I knew that I had got by them one more time.

That was enough bugling until I got to the town.

Finally, the week of the big event arrived. The excitement had reached a feverish pitch. Everybody was dying to see the Princess. Everybody but me, that is. I was just dying—sick as a dog, flat on my back in bed, burning up with fever. Everything on my body ached. My throat was so swollen that I could hardly talk. My nose was so stuffed up that I could hardly breathe. I couldn't have blown the bugle if my life had depended on it. I didn't have enough strength to blow my nose.

But Mom was bound and determined that I was going to be at the train station along with everyone else in town, and that I was going to blow my bugle. She kept me snug in my bed, all day and all night. She poured gallons of chicken broth into me. She stuffed huge gobs of Vicks up my nose. She rubbed my throat and chest with Vicks. She heated towels in the oven, then wrapped them around my throat and crammed them up my pyjamas onto my chest. She kept me sweating like a hog. I knew if I didn't die from the illness, I would certainly die from the cure.

But Mom was a pretty good country doctor, and her treatment worked very well. I wasn't yet a hundred percent, but on the eve of the great event, I was starting to feel much better. In fact, I was well enough to get up and have supper. If things kept improving, I thought, I could even blow a little tune on the old bugle after supper.

"Is Robert going to see the Princess tomorrow?" Gwen asked.

"He certainly is," Mom replied. "He's not that sick that he'd miss the experience of a lifetime. Why, he'd have to be on his deathbed before I'd keep him home at a time like this. He may never get to see a princess again."

"At roll call today, the teacher asked me how he was, and I told her he was still sick," Gwen replied. "Then she said, 'Well, I'm sure he'll be well enough to go and see the Princess tomorrow.' And then Margaret said, 'Oh yeah, well, I hope he's still sick. He always turns all red in the face, trying to blow that dumb horn. But he'll probably be there, with his runny nose, making a fool of himself.'"

"Humph, busybodies," Mom snorted angrily. "The nerve of some people. He has as much right to see the Princess as the teacher or Margaret or anybody else. He'll be there, all right, and if the teacher says anything to you, you tell her to come and talk to me."

Suddenly, I didn't feel so good. Just the thought of Margaret was enough to put me back on my deathbed.

My knees felt weak as I got up from the table, and slowly, like a whipped pup, I slunk back to my bed. If I was going to face the teacher and Margaret before I marched and blew my bugle, I figured I needed another good rub-down and a lot more Vicks.

The next morning was a beautiful morning. It had all the makings of a glorious day—just the kind of a day that a princess would choose for a visit. Mom was so excited, that she had got up long before the birds. I could hear her humming and singing *God Save the King* and *O Canada* long before she called us for breakfast.

I, on the other hand, was still sick as a dog. I had a terrible fever, my head was swimming, I was borderline delirious. I was so dizzy, and my knees were so weak, I couldn't get out of bed.

"Come on, Bobby," Mom sang out, pleading with me. "I think maybe you've just got yourself too worked up. I know that as soon as you get out of bed and dressed, you're going to feel much better. Come on now, this is your big day, remember? You're going to play your bugle for the Princess. You don't want to miss the opportunity of a lifetime, now, do you?"

Finally, the long wait was over. Soon the special train would be arriving and the Princess would be in Edson. The Edson Cadet Corps Drum and Bugle Band assembled right next to the Beanery beside the CNR station. Edsonites and people from near and far turned out in the hundreds. They, too, crowded around the station. They flooded the platform, right up to the line. No one was allowed beyond the line—that was sacred space reserved for the Princess and the town fathers. Everyone was jabbering excitedly, waiting for the special train. Then, in the distance, billowing above the trees, there was the telltale smoke from the smokestack of the old coal-burning steam engine. A few minutes later, the engine appeared. The special train was coming around the bend. A shrill whistle blast cut through the air.

The crowd roared. At last the great day, the unimaginable event, was about to unfold. The Edson Cadet Corps Drum and Bugle Band snapped to attention. First, the drums rolled. Next, the bugles blared—shining so brightly the instructor could see his face in them.

The crowd cheered louder as the engine approached the station. The engineer, caught up in the magic of the moment, laid on the whistle, and the shrill sound drowned out the drums and it drowned out the bugles. It drowned out the roar of the wildly cheering crowd. Mom thought perhaps the old engineer was over doing it just a little—but then, it was not every day an engineer got to bring a special train carrying a real live princess into Edson.

The drums had not finished rolling and the bugles had not finished blaring when the whistle finally died down. But still they could not be heard above the cheering and the yelling of the crowd.

Suddenly, as if by magic, the Princess appeared. She was at the door, at the back of the last car. She smiled and waved. The cheering grew louder, and the crowd waved wildly. The noise rippled away from the station.

Away from Edson. It rolled across the countryside, all the way to the Stump Farm and beyond.

The crowd hushed as the Princess stepped from the train. On the platform, she met the town fathers and their wives. They bowed and curtsied in the approved manner. She inspected the troops, the Edson Cadet Corps Drum and Bugle Band, who stood smartly at attention.

She walked slowly along the platform, smiling and waving at her loyal admirers. The people rejoiced.

Suddenly, there was a gasp from the crowd. The Princess stopped smiling. A strange look crossed her face. She stopped walking. The town fathers stopped walking, too. Their broad smiles had vanished, wiped from their faces. There remained only wide-eyed stares on faces frozen in horror. It was unbelievable. It was unthinkable. And it was happening, horror of all horrors, right in the little town of Edson.

A hand, a little hand had reached out from the crowd, out over the line into the forbidden space, and touched the Princess on the arm. Little fingers tenderly closed, feeling, exploring, confirming that the Princess was indeed a real live person.

When people had collected themselves after this humiliating shock, the Princess was quickly hustled back to the safety of the train. She stopped where she had first appeared, in the door at the back of the last coach. There she turned. A faint smile had returned to her face. It appeared that the Princess had regained her composure after her harrowing experience.

The shrill whistle cut through the air like a knife.

The old steam locomotive chugged. The train started to move. There was a surge of people as everyone crowded forward, closer to the special train. They cheered louder and louder, they waved and they waved as the train slowly pulled away from the station. And the Princess, Princess Elizabeth, our future Queen, stood in the doorway. She waved to the crowd and to the Edson Cadet Corps Drum and Bugle Band. Then the old engine chugged harder, steam hissing, and slowly moved away from the station. As the train picked up speed, the drums rolled and the bugles blared. The crowd cheered as the train raced away down the tracks and disappeared in the distance. In an instant, the crowd fell silent, the drums ceased to roll, and the bugles were mute. And just like that, the Princess was gone.

I have no idea what the topic of conversation was in other households in Edson that evening, but I do know what it was in the log house on the Stump Farm. Mom was in a world of her own. For her, a lifelong dream had come true that day.

"Could you see the Princess okay, Mom?" I asked.

"Oh yes, I could," Mom sighed. Then her eyes got that faraway look and they got all misty. "All my life I've wanted to see a princess, and today I did. Oh, Bobby, she's absolutely gorgeous," Mom continued in her dream world. "She's the most beautiful thing I've ever seen."

The Princess's visit to Edson was now a memory. Was it real? Had she really been to Edson? Was it a dream? One little girl knew for sure. She knew it was not a dream. She had touched the Princess.

"Robert, did you know you're not supposed to touch a princess?" Judy asked me.

"Me? No. Heck, I didn't even know there was such a thing as a real princess," I confessed.

"I didn't either," she sighed.

It was the greatest day in Edson's history, and that's the way it happened.

At least, that's what they tell me. I was sick in bed.

ROBERT J. (B0B) ADAMS

Bob Adams was born in Turner Valley, Alberta in 1938. He grew up in the Edson area, in a log house, built by his father on a farm rich in swamp spruce, tamarack, willows and muskeg.

Bob, an avid outdoorsman, was one of the fortunate few who was able to live his boyhood dreams as he entered the workforce. In 1960, after a number of years with the Alberta Forest Service and Royal Canadian Mounted Police, he began a career with the Provincial Government as a Fish and Wildlife Officer. For the next 33 years, he found his homes to include Brooks, Strathmore, Hinton, Calgary, Peace River and Edmonton.

In 1993, after a full career in Enforcement, he retired from Fish and Wildlife and wrote his first book, The Stump Farm. Today, Bob resides in Edmonton, Alberta with his wife Martha where he continues to work on his writing.

GIVE A "ROBERT J. ADAMS" BOOK TO A FRIEND

Megamy Publishing Ltd.
Box 3507
Spruce Grove, AB T7X 3A7

Send to:

Name:____

Street:____

City:____

Province/ State:________________ Postal/ Zip Code:______________

Please send:

"The Stump Farm"	@ $16.95 = ________
"Beyond the Stump Farm"	@ $16.95 = ________
"Horse Cop"	@ $16.95 = ________
"Fish Cop"	@ $16.95 = ________
"The Elephant's Trunk"	@ $15.95 = ________
"The South Road"	@ $16.95 = ________
"Skunks and Hound Dogs"	@ $16.95 = ________
Shipping and handling per book	@ $ 4.00 = ________
7% GST	= ________
Total amount enclosed:	________

Make cheque or money order payable to:

Megamy Publishing Ltd.

Price subject to change without prior notice.

ORDERS OUTSIDE OF CANADA must be paid in U.S. funds by cheque or money order drawn on U.S. or Canadian Bank.

Sorry no C.O.D.'s.

GIVE A “ROBERT J. ADAMS” BOOK TO A FRIEND

Megamy Publishing Ltd.
Box 3507
Spruce Grove, AB T7X 3A7

Send to:
Name:______________________________

Street:______________________________

City:______________________________

Province/ State:____________ Postal/ Zip Code:__________

Please send:

“The Stump Farm”	@ $16.95 =	________
“Beyond the Stump Farm”	@ $16.95 =	________
“Horse Cop”	@ $16.95 =	________
“Fish Cop”	@ $16.95 =	________
“The Elephant’s Trunk”	@ $15.95 =	________
“The South Road”	@ $16.95 =	________
“Skunks and Hound Dogs”	@ $16.95 =	________
Shipping and handling per book	@ $ 4.00 =	________
	7% GST =	________
	Total amount enclosed:	________

Make cheque or money order payable to:

Megamy Publishing Ltd.

Price subject to change without prior notice.

ORDERS OUTSIDE OF CANADA must be paid in U.S. funds by cheque or money order drawn on U.S. or Canadian Bank.

Sorry no C.O.D.’s.

GIVE A "ROBERT J. ADAMS" BOOK TO A FRIEND

Megamy Publishing Ltd.
Box 3507
Spruce Grove, AB T7X 3A7

Send to:
Name:____________________

Street:____________________

City:____________________

Province/ State:__________ Postal/ Zip Code:__________

Please send:

"The Stump Farm"	@ $16.95 = ______
"Beyond the Stump Farm"	@ $16.95 = ______
"Horse Cop"	@ $16.95 = ______
"Fish Cop"	@ $16.95 = ______
"The Elephant's Trunk"	@ $15.95 = ______
"The South Road"	@ $16.95 = ______
"Skunks and Hound Dogs"	@ $16.95 = ______
Shipping and handling per book	@ $ 4.00 = ______
7% GST	= ______
Total amount enclosed:	______

Make cheque or money order payable to:

Megamy Publishing Ltd.

Price subject to change without prior notice.
ORDERS OUTSIDE OF CANADA must be paid in U.S. funds by cheque or money order drawn on U.S. or Canadian Bank.
Sorry no C.O.D.'s.